I AM REDEEMED

I AM REDEEMED

Phyllis E. Jones Coleman, PhD

AuthorHouse™
1663 Liberty Drive
Bloomington, IN 47403
www.authorhouse.com
Phone: 1-800-839-8640

Published by AuthorHouse 12/03/2012

ISBN: 978-1-4772-8748-4 (sc)
ISBN: 978-1-4772-8749-1 (hc)
ISBN: 978-1-4772-8750-7 (e)

Library of Congress Control Number: 2012920935

CONTENTS

Dedication

I would like to dedicate this book
To my four special ladies, to my daughter who never stop loving
me unconditionally, Tyhisha

To my mother who is deceased, Cleaster Jones
And to my grandmother, Emma Blount and also
To my aunt Nancy, These four ladies of my life always prayed
for me and never gave up on me.

And to my only confidant, my youngest brother, Claude and
to the rest of my siblings, James, Whit and my only sister Patti,
and of course
to my spiritual mother who guides me through life, Vivette
Thomas

And I must not forget my loving husband Leon
Words cannot express the loving gratitude that God has brought us together as one

To all the people who touched my lives and made this book possible . . .

Thank you.

Although my life before Christ was destroyed due to molestation, alcoholism, homelessness, sexual, spousal and drug abuse, God in His love through Christ saw in His redemption plan the new creation-Me!

PREFACE

What on earth, am I here for?

Jeremiah 1:5 (KJV) before I formed thee in the belly I knew thee: and before thou camest forth out of the womb I sanctified thee, and I ordained thee a prophet unto the nations. Before I even was conceived by Albert and Cleaster Jones, God had divine knowledge concerning me because He is omniscient. Psalm 139:4 (KJV) for there is not a word in my tongue but, lo, O LORD: thou knows it all together. He tailored design me as one of His' original masterpiece. God has put me together in a way that can't and should not be replicated. He chose every aspect of my personality, crafted every gift and talent He bestowed on me, and gave special thoughts to each one of my features and traits. I was hand made by Him in my mother's womb. His custom—designed me to fit a specific role in His sovereign plan. Through the Lord Jesus Christ

I have been brought with a price. 1 Corinthians 6:19-20 (NIV) Do you not know that your temple of the Holy Spirit, who is in you, whom you have received from?

You are your not own; 20) you were bought at a price. Therefore honor God with your body.

The Word of God states in 1Peter 1:2 (NIV) "Who have been chosen according to the foreknowledge of God the Father, through the sanctifying work of the Spirit, for obedience to Jesus Christ and sprinkling by his blood: Grace and peace be yours in abundance." Even before I was born, God had sanctified (set me apart) for His' glory. Through the Lord as a believer I must maintain intimate communion with Christ. John 15:4 (TLB) state Remain in me and I will remain in you. For a branch cannot produce fruit if it is severed from the vine, and you cannot be fruitful apart from me. Through the Lord I must continue to engage in fellowship with believers. Ephesians 4:15-16 (KJV) state "But speaking the truth in love, may grow up into in all things which is the head even Christ: 16) From whom the whole body fitly joined together and compacted by that which every joint supplieth, according to the effectual working in the measure of every part, maketh increase of the body unto the edifying itself in love. Through the Lord I must continue to devote myself in prayer. Colossians 4:2 (NIV) Devote yourselves to prayer being watchful and thankful. Through the Lord I must continue to obey God's Word. John 17:17 (NIV) Sanctify them by the truth; your word is truth. Through the Holy Spirit I must remain sensitive to

God's presence and care. Mathew 6:25-34 (NIV) "Therefore I tell you do not worry about your life, what you will eat or drink, or about your body, what you will wear. Is not life more important than food, and the body more important than clothes? 26 Look at the birds of the air, they do not sow or reap or store away of you in barns and yet your heavenly Father feeds them. Are you not much more valuable than they? 27 Who of you by worrying can add a single hour to his life? 28 And why do you worry about clothes? See how the lilies of the field grow. They do Not labor or spin. 29 Yet I tell that not even Solomon in all his splendor was dressed like one of these. 30 If that is how God clothes the grass of the field, which is here today and tomorrow is thrown into the fire, will he not much more clothe you. O you faith? 31 So do not worry, saying, 'What shall we eat?' or 'What shall we drink?' or'What shall we wear?' 32 For the pagan run after all these things, and you're heavenly Father knows that you need them. 32 But seek first his kingdom and righteousness, and all these things will be given to as well. 34

Therefore do not worry about tomorrow, for tomorrow will worry about itself. Each day has enough trouble of its own. God has command me to love righteousness and hate wickedness. Hebrew 1:9 (NIV) state you have loved righteousness and hated wickedness, therefore God have you above your companions by anointing you with the oil of joy.

Through Christ my old self has been crucified (put sin to death) with Christ on the cross in order that I might believe and receive a new life in Christ. Romans 6:6 (NIV) states that for we know that our old was crucified with him so that the body of sin might be done away with that we should no longer be slaves to sin. So bless it be the name of the Lord! The word of God state that in Romans 6:7&11 (NIV) because anyone Phyllis E. Jones who has died has been freed from sin. In the same way count yourselves dead to sin but alive to God in Christ Jesus.

Through Christ, He has given me the divine power of Him to resist sin. So I can live a new life in obedience to God. Through Him I can continue to obey, and be filled with the Holy Spirit. Romans 8:14 (NIV) state that because those who led by the Spirit of God are son of God. Ephesians 5:18 (NIV) Do not get drunk with wine, which leads to debauchery. Instead be filled with the Spirit. Even before I was born God ordained me, He had appointed me, and He called me to the Great Commission. Mathew 28:18-20 (NIV) Then Jesus came to them and said, "All authority in heaven and earth has been given to me. I Phyllis E. Jones therefore must go and make disciples of all nations, baptizing them in the name of the Father and of the Son and of the Holy Spirit, 20 teaching them to obey everything I have commanded you. And surely I am with you always, to the age. God has given me divine authority set the captive free. Isaiah 61:1-3 (NIV)

The Spirit of the Sovereign Lord is on me (Phyllis E. Jones), because the Lord has anointed me to preach good news to the poor. He has sent me to bind up the brokenhearted, to proclaim freedom for captives and release from darkness for the prisoners, 2 to proclaim the year of the Lord's favor and the vengeance of our God, to comfort all who mourn, and provide for those who grieve in Zion—to bestow on them a crown of beauty instead of ashes, the oil of gladness instead of mourning, and a garment of praise instead of a spirit of despair. They will be called oaks of righteousness, a planting of the Lord for the display of his splendor.

So in conclusion of this question what on earth, am I here for? God knew (approved) me and sanctified me (set me apart), and ordained (commissioned) me before I was even born. Smith Wiggle worth quotes "God has a plan beyond anything that we have ever known. He has a plan for every individual life, and if we have any other plan in view, we miss the grandest plan of all. Nothing in the past is equal to the present, and nothing in the present can equal the things of tomorrow. Tomorrow should be filled with holy expectations that we will be living flames for Him. God never intended His people to be ordinary or commonplace. His intentions were that they should be on fire for Him, conscious of His divine power, realizing the glory of the Cross that foreshadows the crown." This is the desire God has given me

What was your divine purpose at birth?

Ephesians 1:4-5 (NIV) "For he chose us in him before the creation of the world to be holy and blameless in his sight. In love he predestined us to be adopted as his sons through Jesus Christ, in accordance with his pleasure and will." God divine purpose for my life even before I was born, He foreknew from eternity was to love and redeem me through Christ. As a believer I must maintain my faith in Christ so that I will not fall short of His glorification.

The election to salvation and holiness of the body of Christ is always certain. Christ, as the elect, is the foundation of my election. It is only in union with Christ that I became a member of the elect. Isaiah 42:1 (NIV) "Here is my servant, whom I uphold, my chosen one in whom I delight, I will put my Spirit on him and he will bring justice to the nations. Through the power of the Holy Spirit, Jesus was raised from the grave and thereby vindicated as the true Messiah and the Son of God. Just as Jesus depended on the Holy Spirit for his resurrection, I as a believer must continue to depend on the Holy Spirit for spiritual life now and bodily resurrection in the future. It is only through the anointing of the Holy Spirit I can minister with the necessary wisdom, revelation and power. Isaiah 44:1-2 (NIV) But now listen, O Jacob, my servant, Israel, whom I have chosen. 2 This is what the Lord says—he who made you, who formed you in the womb, and who will help you. God chose me even before

I was born be to a servant of the Most High God. Lucifer knew I was mark by God, so he tried everything in his power to destroy me and to kill me. I thank God each day because what Lucifer tried for evil, but being a chosen vessel God had a divine purpose for my life. He brought me up from the grave,

He spared me from going down into the pit. He has turned my weeping into rejoicing. He has turned my wailing into dancing, He removed my sackcloth and He has clothed with His' joy. That my heart may sing to Him and not be silent. I will thank the Lord for rest of my life. God has taught me that I was born to glorify Him. Christ will present me "holy and blameless in sight "only if I continue in faith.

I thank God; He has predestined me as one of His elect to be: Romans 8:30 (NIV) state that and those he predestined, he also called, those he called, he also justified, those he also justified, he also glorified. Romans 8:29(NIV) states that For those God foreknew he also predestined to be conformed to the likeness of his Son, that he might be the firstborn among many brothers. He also predestine as one of His elect to be Ephesians 1:4(NIV) for he chose Phyllis E. Jones in him before the creation of the world to be holy and blameless in his sight. 5 he predestines me Phyllis E. Jones to be adopted as his daughter through Jesus Christ in accordance with his good pleasure and will 6 to the praise of his glorious grace which he has given Phyllis E. Jones in the One he loves. I thank God, He has redeemed through His blood. Ephesian 1:7 (NIV) state in him I have redemption through his blood, the forgiveness of sin, in accordance with the riches of God's grace. Ephesians 2:10 (NIV) state For I Phyllis E. Jones is God's workmanship created in Christ Jesus to do good works which God prepared in advance for me to do.

Donald C. Stamp quotes "Concerning election and predestination, we might use the Analogy of a great ship on its way to heaven. The ship (church) is chosen by God to be his very own vessel. Christ is the Captain and Pilot of this ship.

All who desire to be a part of this elect ship and its Captain can do so through a living faith in Christ, by which they come on board the ship. As long as they are on the ship, in company with ship's Captain, they are among the elect. If they choose to abandon the ship and Captain, they cease to be part of the elect. Election is always only in union with the Captain and his ship. Predestination tells us about the ship's destination and what God has prepared for those remaining on it. God invites everyone to come aboard the elect ship through faith in Jesus Christ.

What is the seed of God?

God has given me a vision to open a women discipleship Christ center program. The population of women the Spirit of the Lord is directing me to disciple are: women with life controlling problems women who AIDS or HIV diagnosis women who have substance abuse issues Lord willing, one I would like do one on one Christian Counseling/Psychology Practice.

What is my hell and why don't you go through your night season? My hell is procrastination and at times the fear of the unknown. Proverb 20:4 (NIV) states The lazy man will not plow because of winter; he will beg during harvest and have nothing. Also 2 Timothy 1:7 (NIV) God did not give us a spirit of fear but of love power and a sound mind. I must continue trust in the Lord with all of my heart and lean not on my own understanding and acknowledge Him all of my ways and HE shall direct my path.

Preface

The Bible condemns drunkenness and alcohol abuse but makes no specific reference to drug abuse, eating disorders, workaholics, or most other addictions that concern us today. In many societies, thousands of individuals are addicted to alcohol, drugs, television, compulsive spending, sexual immorality, smoking, overeating and a host of other behaviors.

An addiction is anything or a behavior that is habitual, repetitious and difficult or impossible to control. Usually the addiction brings short-term pleasure, but there may be long-term consequences in terms of one's health and welfare. Addictions tend to be progressive conditions that slowly exert more and more power and control over the individual.

As people move from infancy toward maturity, they travel through developmental periods in which people have somewhat similar characteristics. Each individual advances through various stages in life-all distinctly different-to maturity. The infant stage differs greatly from the junior high, but both contribute to the total development in the life span of the individual.

For the Christian there are two aspects of personality developments. One relates to the natural human personality and the other is the Christian personality. Personality, in the natural human sense, is a term describing the total of what people are physically, intellectually, socially, emotionally and spiritually. It includes every aspect and area of life.

From birth personality is influenced and molded by many forces, heredity and environment being the major forces. Within the environment, mainly family, school, church, peer group and society influence a person.

Subsequent, physical, intellectual, emotional, social and spiritual structure is built upon the foundation of early childhood. Growth and development are not synonymous terms. Growth means to increase in size, function and complexity up to maturity. Development implies change over time in structure, thought and behavior caused by biological and environmental influences.

As the individual experience the human development from birth to adulthood, the addicted too must endure to achieve redemption from the bondage of sin for God always takes us back to the root of the situation. Thereby, the elementary stage is evident when one begins God's process of redemption.

God planned our Redemption. His Son and the Holy Spirit executed it. This redemption demonstrated the eternal defeat of Satan. Jesus stripped him of his authority and dominion after He had paid the penalty of man's transgression.

INTRODUCTION

My life before redemption was pure hell; yet, God's plan, unknowingly to me, was already in process. My only sister tells me later that while she was at work, sitting at the computer, she was endowed with heaviness from a vision. As she sat there, the burden increased, thoughts of me growing stronger as the tears began to flow, uncontrollably. Finally after seeking privacy-thank God the office she shared with 8 other women was empty, she got up; God had chose lunchtime.

She proceeded to the rest room and began to wail-God had released the tearless anguish of me the oldest and only sister on her (Jeremiah 9:17). Time was not of the essence because God had known my heart; my sister felt my pain and thereby God had prepared the baby and only sister for the deliverance. She was to stand in the gap for my redemption, "I looked for a man among them who would build up the wall and stand before me in the gap on behalf of the land so I would not have to destroy it" Ezekiel 22:30 (NIV). She had made herself available for God. The opportunity was presenting itself and God's plan for my redemption was being enforced.

Even though, I always strayed away, my sister would find me if she had not seen me for 2 - 3 months. She basically knew the area-would always start where I was last found; she loved me. One quest, in particular, began under the inspiration of the Holy Spirit. My sister again went to the area searched with persistence. Finally, there I was in a terrible condition. I normally kept myself neat and tidy, hair in place. But now, to her amazement-the body was very frail, hair covered by a scarf-discovered later to be matted. I asked her for money. She would not have that and advised me to go to our maternal grand aunt. Giving me money was a no, no to her. She knew what I wanted it for as I begged and pleaded with her because I was sickly in need of a fix. She also knew that she would be accountable to God if that one fix she paid for brought harm to me; my blood would be on her hands. In her heart, she felt oh my God; yet, she remembered God had shown her my redemption.

The two of us talked-the message from God (the vision) was delivered; she took me to our aunt's. Shortly after, she left grieving inside-not wanting to leave. She knew that it was not God's time. For the next visit, she promised to return on my birthday to take me to dinner.

At dinner, talk was limited-I was too high, higher than I would have ever let my baby sister see me. But God! There I sat at one of the most influential restaurants in town; God knew I loved shrimp and lobster only the respect I exercised for her in not seeing me high could not be controlled; on occasion I nodded. Ever so be it, the seeds were planted-how much God loved me; that I was beautiful, fearfully and wonderfully made (Ps. 139:14); how Christ died that I might live in Him. Although, there was a battle in gaining my attention, my sister had faith.

Visits continued wherever I strayed. The very last place she saw me, was horrific-no running water, no lights, no heat, sewer backed up and so on. The attempt for survival was inevitable. The older brother had visited from out of state insisting on finding me-he was in need of drugs; he knew I could get them. Our baby sister pretended to see nothing, but inside she grieved, as it were both of us-the older brother and myself were addicted to heroine. Sometime later, the house was condemned; I would wait until night, sneak back in, and sleep on the floor under the carpet. All along, the devil was telling me I was nothing, would never be nothing, to go ahead and kill myself; he actually wanted me to commit suicide. Eventually it became too cold, for winter had come; I would go and sit in the emergency room of the local hospital. I was homeless.

God's redemptive plan was still in motion. While at the hospital, I inquired of the Substance Abuse Detoxification Program. What would normally take days for admittance, I was told to be back by 2:30 pm. God opened the door and I went in. I received a physical. I took a shower. After receiving my bed, I laid around waiting for my first dose of medication; by this time, everyone else had received his or hers.

One only knows what I was experiencing at this time; I was a drug addict and I needed the medication. One of the other patients attempted to assist me to the Nurse's Station to inquire about the medication; however, I was too weak to make it. We turned around and I returned to bed. My temperature was taken; I had a fever of 104. And then I cried out, "Lord, Lord Have Mercy On Me! I was given some water; I felt the release of which I know now of that demon of suicide leaving the pit of my stomach. I fell asleep; I later discovered the flash I had a dining room was the Teen Challenge dining room.

Finally, my sister received a call from our maternal grand aunt who had seen me at this particular hospital. My sister began making telephone calls to find out what was going on. Not able to get much information-only that I was there over the telephone, she decided to make an appointment at the hospital. Upon her visit, the doctor articulated that he had begun the detoxification process on me. He also stated that he was using great caution-my situation was just that bad. He advised her that she could not see me; however, she would be his point of contact.

Fourteen days later, the call came-the detoxification was successfully completed. The caller inquired, "Where will she live?" The reply, "She could live with me." My sister was informed that it took longer than usual for the detoxification, had it been rushed I could have died-my dependency on the heroine was just that great. But God had a plan for my redemption-death was not His will!

Living with my sister and my mother was very different; this was a Christian home. Secular music, smoking, cussing, alcohol nor coming in all times of night was allowed. Not only was it the holy lifestyle she had chosen to live, the home was a safe-haven for our mother whose life God had spared ten years prior; evil did not reign in this home.

My sister worked Monday through Friday-everyday she would leave a biblical assignment for me. After work, we'd sit; she'd take the time to discuss the material and minister the assignment expecting feedback with the assurance that I understood what God's Word was saying. This went on for a while until . . . . our grand aunt's companion died. This took the two of us back up north where God had brought me. During the trip, it was suggested that I refrain from any alcohol, I agreed. Our return back home proved that the environment was unhealthy-I had snuck and had a beer. The enemy in me stuck his head up and I cursed my sister out, threatened to burn the house down with our disabled mother in it. I left and didn't return that night. My sister was not moved. There was still hope. The very next day at work, she consulted with a co-worker whom she had been having Bible Study with-he was a Pastor. The two of them went into her new office and began to intercede.

Prayer does change the condition of things! It was discovered later that at the same time they were praying, I was overwhelmed with a warm sensation; mind you, I had just taken a hit of heroine, drank a beer and smoked a cigarette. The warm sensation wasn't from the initial rush you get when shooting heroine; no, no, that was the Holy Spirit inspiring to call my sister. I did just that! The Holy Spirit was telling me to leave where I was. By this time, the Holy Spirit had spoken to her; I needed long-term help of which she conveyed to me; I agreed. She inquired to be sure that I was not doing this based on the alternative given-either I go into a Christian rehab or I had to leave the home. What tough love! I assured her I was doing it for myself, for God.

The Pastor had given her information of the Teen Challenge Ladies Home-a Christian facility of which she contacted. She was advised that a call had to come from me to prove my readiness; I made the call. They had a bed! This place normally had a waiting list; but God! Thereafter, preparations were made to meet the requirements for my admission. I needed a medical examination, certain clothing, a bible, toiletries, etc. I was taken to her beautician and treated with royalty; my sister confided in her beautician of my condition expecting the utmost services for me-it took two hours for the shampoo girl to untangle my hair in order to receive a permanent relaxer! God blessed my sister to be able to pay all expenses necessary for my entry to include the admission fee. My sister remained involved for the next 16 months of a 12 months program.

CHAPTER ONE

THE BEGINNING

"As a rule, at the Teen Challenge Ladies Home, you aren't allowed visitors for the first three months. For me this did not happen until much later; my spiritual deliverance from certain demons was brutal and lengthy. The requirement of successful completion of each phase and written documentation of each level, section is mandatory. This is the beginning of God's process for MY REDEMPTION!

The Scriptures And The Addict

"Accepting Jesus Christ as Lord and Savior can stop drug addiction. The things I did I hated and it made a big effect on my life. But the sins I did, dwelled in me. I didn't understand. I learned to first go to the heart and address it with scripture. I found out what sinning was. Anyone who deals with Christ is a new creature. Eventually, God will take away the pain. And all things will past away. And upon my salvation, He will forgive me. And most of all through *new birth of the praise of the Lord, I finally learned! You do not sin because you are an addict. You are an addict because of sinning!*

By my accepting Christ in my life, I discovered I wasn't sinning because I was an addict; I was an addict because I was sinning. I didn't understand. My eyes were opening pertaining to the scripture, the Word of Christ. There I found out what sinning is. I am truly astonished. I have learned to first go to the heart and address it with scripture. My heart has been enlightened.

I thought it was the environment; but it is all over. By escaping your personality, you inherit emotional hang-ups. With the rejections and personal hang-ups, I became a sinner. I began to put the blame on someone else, some times my parents (challenged parental responsibilities), and sometimes my siblings. My self-confidence was in drugs and alcohol. The reality was I was not a sinner because of the addiction; I was an addict because of the sin. Personally, I had to relax myself, trust in God, give Him more praises and believe in Jesus."

"I do not understand what I do. For what I want to do I do not do, but what I hate I do. As it is, it is no longer I myself who do it, but it is sin living in me"

Romans 7:15&17 (NIV).

"Jesus answered, "I am the way and the truth and the life. No one comes to the Father except through me"

John 14:6 (NIV).

Sin has always fooled people by misusing the law. When Eve encountered the serpent in the Garden of Eden (Genesis 3), the serpent fooled her by taking her focus off the freedom God had given her and putting it on the one restriction He had made. Ever since then, we have all been rebels. Sin looks good to us precisely because God has said it is bad. Instead of paying attention to his warnings, we use them as a "to do" list. When we feel rebellious, we need to back off and look at the law from a wider perspective-in light of God's grace and mercy. If we focus on His great love for us, we will understand why He asks us to restrict our behavior. He only restricts us from things that ultimately will harm us.

We must never underestimate the power of sin. Satan is a crafty tempter and we have a great ability to make excuses. Instead of trying to overcome sin with human will power, we must take hold of the tremendous power of Christ that is available to us. This is God's provision for victory over sin; He sends the Holy Spirit to live in us and give us power. And when we fall, He lovingly reaches out to us and helps us up.

"The devil made me do it;" it sounds like a lame excuse, but it may be true. Without Christ's help, sin is stronger than we are, and sometimes we are unable to defend ourselves against its attacks. That is why we should never stand up to sin all alone. Jesus Christ, who has conquered sin once and for all, promises to fight by our side. If we look to him for help, we will not have to give in to sin.

It is false that anyone who is good and innocent will never suffer. The Bible gives us teachings and examples of what we should do as well as what we should not do. The Bible teaches that everyone has a natural tendency to sin. Those who follow God, however, can decide to resist sin.

The Bible is not an end in itself, but a means to bring men to an intimate and satisfying knowledge of God, that they may enter into Him, that they may delight in His presence, may taste and know the inner sweetness of the very God Himself in the core and center of their hearts. God brings understanding with truth. He is the one who actually preserves the truth in us. The sinner that became the drug addict went astray. The root of the problem was that the sinner needed the Lord Jesus; didn't have the strength to do well for in the flesh dwells no good thing.

Many that are delivered from drug addiction and alcoholism struggle with patterns; some perish with in the sin. The habit becomes an addiction caused by a private pattern caused by a habitual sin. Many that give their life to Christ often return to their sinful ways. Why do some go back? The addict must know that upon salvation we receive forgiveness. The Law of Principles: 1st Adam (old nature)-bondage & last Adam (new creature)-deliverance; the addict no longer has to be bound by drugs any longer.

Deliverance wasn't from the drugs for the drug addict. Deliverance was from sins to acceptance of Jesus Christ as Savior. No need to call out demons but deal with God first. So it is written: "The first man Adam became a living being;" the last Adam, a life-giving spirit. The first man was of the dust of the earth, the second man from heaven" (1 Corinthians 15:45 (NIV). All that are by faith united to Christ are by his resurrection given assurance. As through the sin of the first Adam, all men became mortal, because all had from him the same sinful nature, so, through the resurrection of Christ, shall all who are made to partake of the Spirit, and the spiritual nature, revive, and live forever.

The Father Heart Of God

"Everyone has emotional wounds and pain that can only be healed by God. The way we can be healed is to ask God for forgiveness. You should believe and trust in Him. We should let go of our pride and just give ourselves to God. Our God is a forgiving God. He will do anything but fail. We should always be patient and to continue to have faith in Him. God uses family problems and emotional wounds to show He is able to heal. Through different processes, ones are healed. He expressed healing by using my family problems and emotional wounds, causing them to surface.

God's healing power, love and compassion enabled me to overcome some very painful experiences. We must let go of pride, believe, trust and submit ourselves unto Him. We should always be patient and continue to have faith in Him. God is good. His character is Creator, Provider, Friend, Counselor, Corrector, Redeemer, Comforter, Defender Deliverer and/or Redeemer. God is forgiving, kind and loving as a Father. He can do anything but fail. God can do anything as long as you surrender. You get to know Him personally by believing He sacrificed His Son Jesus Christ who came to forgive us from our sins.

My life has been enriched by God's unchanging heart. His 24 hours daily affection is pursued with compassion when I hurt. God's presence is always there. God's unconditional love is acceptable. He is love and He loves us just the way we are. You must always pray; we should learn how to communicate with Him to know how God is. Ask to be forgiven and forgive others."

"Have mercy on me, O God, according to your unfailing love; according to your great compassion blot out my transgressions" Psalm 51:1 (NIV).

Many people never experience a real relationship with their natural father. With some, it is because the father does not live in their home. Many others have fathers who live in their home but, for one reason or another, either cannot or will not show affection for their children. As a result, many people never feel a father's love.

God is not to be judged by our human experiences of a father. The natural father was a man who failed in many ways; he had weaknesses as well as strengths. Many children have suffered rejection at the hands of their human fathers, because they were men who could not be trusted. They were unjust or unconcerned about their children. God never abuses His children. He is near to all who call on Him. He is never distant. God comforts, strengthens and heals His children. The Great I AM That I AM is not to be compared with any other father.

The world is plagued with pain. Many have been pushed to the trenches of society's rejection. I have discovered no level of society is immune from pain of broken relationships, anger, resentment, rejection and a negative childhood; all of which can hold back understanding of God as a Father. God's authority is His goodness. We lacked this authority by not trusting. But God is the only one we can trust and He never fails. Mankind's value of things is priceless to God's tangible forgiveness, mercy and love.

God' plan of redemption is enforced by a process of sanctification when you are hurting of emotions, rescued from sin and selfishness. It brings healing for both guilt and the self-centeredness. Those in mourning are given the "oil of gladness" (Isaiah 61:3).

When the heart is wounded with results ending in inferiority, independence, pride, fear of man, disobedience, manipulation, withdrawal, impatience, distrust, disloyalty, ingratitude and unhealthy idealism better known as the "Saul syndrome," mending is costly. There is a great price to pay if you want to experience God's inner healing and to know the Father's love; you must choose the fear of the Lord.

The following must be considered in order for God to heal your emotions: you must first be honest; confess your sins; repent; ask for forgiveness; admit the need to receive God's grace. You must trust in the Lord; build a heart to heart relationship with God-disassociation leads to further pain and emotional injury. You must confess your negative emotion-some Christians do not show emotions.

God created us to live a balanced life of expression and enjoyment of our emotions with freedom to deal honestly and constructively. Every problem of disunity can be solved with greater humility or forgiveness. Forgive those who hurt you. Receive forgiveness always confess to God your sins. Receive the Father's love. Spend time in His presence. Think godly thoughts whenever you think of negative thoughts; think God's way. Endure the beginning, struggle gain the friendship with God. God is a Healer. God is Loving and Compassionate. God's heart is unchanging.

We should never put our focus for healing on people as the source of healing in our lives. If you want an individual to heal you, you will be disappointed. Disappointment positions you for hurt along with discouragement, bitterness, anger unbelief and fear. Effects of disappointment can linger for months or years, hindering our relationship with our Father God; the reaction determines a moral and a spiritual choice, which can influence one's life forever.

Many people, in the world, haven't any understanding of a God who is a loving Father. God knows the pain of a broken heart. By denying His existence, men and women deny the ultimate meaning to life itself and therefore deny the basis of saying it is wrong for people to suffer.

We know our hearts; we must examine our response to evil and suffering. Godly grief produces a repentance that leads to salvation and brings no regret, but worldly grief produces death. Most of us suffer, to some extent from low self-image with emotional wounds; the temptation is great to become a self-centered person.

When we have sinned greatly, after all the waiting the Father does, He still forgives us. He has an unconditional acceptance giving us the freedom to choose; this freedom can be violated if we do not give other people the same freedom God give us. God is a God of patience and waits to meet our every need; He awaits us to be gracious.

The need for balance, emphasis on spiritual fathering, can be carried to the extreme. Mankind often reduces God to their level. Biblical authority is never taken; it is offered. It does not reside in a position or a right. Absolute obedience is given only to God; submission is given to man. Submission involves an attitude of openness to receive from someone else. God is the only one worthy of total allegiance.

CHAPTER TWO

PREPARING OUR SELF FOR SPIRITUAL CHANGE

"When I gave my life to Christ, I was tired of living a sinful life and knew of no other help. No flesh could heal my body (I discovered in a year ago that I was sick); so, I yielded to Christ to do the work in me. I'm becoming more stable in the Lord. I am able to think better and smile more. I'm also getting my salvation back-when the person becomes saved.

Change is painful. I choose not to be like some people who would rather die than change. I must accept the change. I never knew how badly I'd sinned until the process for my redemption began, the upward climb. At times, I feel like a yo-yo Christian; sometimes up and sometimes down without consistency. Stability comes with change. When I decided to let the Lord change me for my marriage, work and ministry, I began to be stable, established in life.

As long as I am active with prayer, the Holy Spirit remains. I feel safe and protected in the arms of Jesus. I am at ease with knowing where I am going (eternity). The Lord is delivering me day by day; I am experiencing the cleansing from emotional wounds such as, attitude, resentment and anger that had opened the door to the devil.

What has brought me out of this entirely? A friend called God! God is sovereign, now I'm somebody. Hurt as a child, God put safety around me. As long as Jesus is my friend, I don't need anyone else. I can talk to Him anytime. I cry to him anytime. I thank him all the time. No matter what, I trust in God with all of my heart and believe He will make a way. There is nothing that I cannot do because Jesus gives me the strength.

However, I must forgive everybody who I thought hurt me in the past. I am choosing to be different than many I watch-they don't pray nor read scriptures. They stay at home on Sundays and not go to church. Their day is spent watching television allowing the TV to bring the world into their homes. They are yet to be saved from the wrath of God.

Everyone has different motives; some are searching for God as a friend but don't know how to grasp him. I must be understanding and listen to them. I must be ready to minister what the Lord has done in my life, to help everyone-different nationalities and backgrounds.

Looking to God in search for answers to emptiness is a part of the process for my redemption; this will definitely help bring me out of the fiery furnace. Giving of myself to Christ provides me with many other chances as long as I live. Christians backslide because they want their own way for the rules, according to which all ought to walk and act, the commandments given by God through Jesus Christ.

The Book of Revelations mentions the seal on the forehead: "And out of the smoke locusts came down upon the earth and were given power like that of scorpions of the earth. They were told not to harm the grass of the earth or any plant or tree, but only those people who did not have the seal of God on their foreheads. They were not given power to kill them, but only to torture them for five months. And the agony they suffered was like that of the sting of a scorpion when it strikes a man" Revelation 9:3-5 (NIV); versus the presence of the Holy Spirit (oil) anointing: "You prepare a table before me in the presence of my enemies. You anoint my head with *oil; my cup overflows" Psalm 23:5 (NIV). I must desire to have Jesus as my Savior. Sometimes people can be saved by a testimony. Giving my life to Christ has made a big difference. The Holy Spirit is now helping me to control my motives and emotions. The Holy Spirit is guiding me in the correct manner to walk. The Holy Spirit is causing me not to sin; I have a conscience of the right way. As long as I have Jesus Christ as my Savior, I am able to live right. I will be prosperous and successful; He will open the doors for me. As long as I have God in my life, I will be all right. God is real; He's good and worthy to be praised."*

"May God himself, the God of peace, sanctify you through and through. May your whole spirit, soul and body be kept blameless at the coming of our Lord Jesus Christ" 1 Thessalonians 5:23 (NIV).

Sanctification is the renewal of the soul under the influences of the Holy Spirit with attention to appointed duties, constituting the will of God in respecting them. In aspiring after this renewal of the soul unto holiness, strict restraint must be placed upon the appetites and senses of the body and the thoughts and inclinations of the will which leads to wrong usage of them. The Lord calls none into His family to live unholy lives; ones are taught and given the ability to walk before Him in holiness.

Becoming a Christian is a spiritual transformation; God works the new birth in everyone's life through the process of sanctification to change our lives. With this kind of a change, the flesh is controlled. Throughout the process, God brings soundness (wholeness).

Jesus promised the ministry of the Holy Spirit (Spirit of Promise): "If you love me, you will obey what I command. And I will ask the Father, and he will give you another Counselor to be with you forever—the Spirit of Truth. The world cannot accept him, because it neither sees him nor knows him. But you know him, for he lives with you and will be in you. I will not leave you as orphans; I will come to you. Before long, the world will not see me anymore, but you will see me. Because I live, you also will live. On that day, you will realize that I am in my Father, and you are in me, and I am in you. Whoever has my commands and obeys them, he is the one who loves me. He who loves me will be loved by my Father, and I too will love him and show myself to him" John 15:15-20 (NIV).

As it were, John the Baptist was sent as the messenger in preparation for Christ; God the Father sends His Spirit to prepare us to be Christ's temple. We are the temples of the Holy Ghost. He cleanses our temple from the inside out. If we appear to be able to endure (endurance is having God), the Lord takes us through many more different channels. The "going through" trials and tribulations is just a test of assurance-do you really want Jesus Christ as your Savior and the abundant reward that He brings?

The more pure and holy the heart becomes, the stronger the ability to sense the remaining strongholds. The excellence of the law, the beauty of holiness becomes visual. The earnest desire to obey increases with growth. As the believer is under grace, his life of holiness (righteous conduct) is more sincere. The inward man-that new man in him is then re-created in true holiness.

Find The Treasure In You

"God is telling me, He doesn't want me to put myself down. I didn't believe God loved me when I first came to Teen Challenge-I had to wait until January to celebrate Christmas. I didn't realize that God has given me so many strengths that He wishes to use. As a Christian, I should want to be like Jesus. I asked God to make me any way He wants according to His way and will. I must allow God to have His way. I must first accept myself as I am and then recognize my faults. God will make me sturdy again. God desires for me to be the best in everything I do or say.

God accepts me but I must accept myself as a sinner. The image of God, in me, was damaged when I sinned. I have a choice of being good or bad. I must believe God sees me when I fall short of His glory. God uses weak people to make them strong. As a Christian, I become the temple of the Holy Spirit. So, I must be obedient as a child of God. I am here for a good purpose-to become like Jesus. My self-image had a big effect on my life; I needed to be loved, accepted, to feel I belonged. I needed to be confident and to do things well. My self-image rested on these."

"But let it be the hidden man of the heart, in that which is not corruptible, even the ornament of a meek and quiet spirit, which is in the sight of God of great price" 1 Peter 3:4 (KJV).

We are reflections of God's image. God is sinless, eternal, and unlimited. Although we are given the potential to be sinless and eternal, we are also given the choice to fall short. We will never be totally like God, because He is our supreme Creator. Our best hope is to reflect His character in our love, patience, forgiveness, kindness, and faithfulness.

We are made like God and therefore share many of His characteristics and emotions. Knowing this provides the basis for self-worth. Self-worth is not defined by possessions, achievements, physical attractiveness, or public acclaim; self-worth knows that God created us in His likeness. Criticizing or downgrading ourselves is criticizing what God has made. Because we are like God, we can feel positive about our abilities and ourselves. Knowing that you are a person of infinite worth gives you the freedom to love God, know Him personally and make a valuable contribution to those around us.

Let us consider, first of all, the nature of this self-life. Self is the power with which God has created and endowed every being. It is the very center of a created being. And why did God give the angels and man a self? The object of this self was that we might bring it as an empty vessel unto Him-that He might put into it His life giving us the power of self-determination, that we might surrender this self every day.

God wanted a vessel into which He might pour out His divine fullness of beauty, wisdom and power. And so, He created the world, the sun, the moon, the stars, the trees, the flowers and the grass, which all show forth the riches of His wisdom, beauty and goodness. But, they do it without knowing what they do.

Then, God created the angels with a self and a will, to see whether they would come and voluntarily yield themselves to Him as vessels for Him to fill. This was not done; not all did that. There was one at the head of a great company who began to look upon self, thinking of the wonderful power with which God had endowed him and delighted in himself. He exalted himself; pride asserted itself in separation from God and that very moment he became instead of an angel in heaven, a devil in hell. Self-turned away from God is the very darkness and fire of hell; self-turned to God is the glory of allowing the Creator to reveal Himself in us.

Self-will and self-exaltation is the works of self. Self-will, pleasing self, is the great sin of man; it is the root of all compromising to the world and the ruin of so many. The world has yet to understand why they should not please themselves and do their own will; as well as, the number of Christians that have never grasped the concept that a Christian is never to seek his own will but is always to seek the will of God; he should be the vessel in whom the very Spirit of Christ lives.

We find Christians pleasing themselves in a thousand ways and yet trying to be happy, good and useful without knowing that the self-will is at the root of it all, robbing them of the blessing. Self-pleasing is the cause of this self and denies Jesus. It must be one of the two; either the Christian please Jesus—Him only and deny self, or please self and deny Jesus. This self started from hell, separated us from God and is the cursed deceiver that leads us astray from Jesus.

Sad Childhood Experience

"When I was a child I could never understand why I didn't have a father. Then when I got a little older I had to accept responsibilities-never being able to play with my friends. When I became 12 years old a relative molested me; I couldn't understand why he took my virginity away

so young. At the time, I did not know that this would be one of my biggest sins; it caused me to drug it.

My father left my mother alone all by herself with five children, two before and two after me. I was born of 5 children; I can remember my mother had to raise us by herself. I know today and I believe I was born of rejection because my father took my mother through hell. I believe my mother didn't want me. But she didn't abort me. I used to ask did my mother want me. She never mistreated me; she was always a mother who forbids her children to talk back to their elders-I do have a fear of talking.

My maternal grandfather's death made me very rebellious toward my childhood life. My maternal grandmother's death really made me confused; why would the Lord take away someone I really loved? I began smoking and drinking at the age of 13. I never had a childhood life of happiness. From that day on I drugged almost every day for it took away the pain until four months ago. Heroine had been my drug of choice, then pills, cocaine and alcohol.

In the absence of my father and in relationships with others, I took to some of my friends as a father. This is why most of my life I dealt with older men. I had always wanted a father like my girlfriends. I felt rejected not having a father all of my life! At the age of 40, I still miss the presence of my father. My father left me at the age of five or four years old.

For many years, all my life I held the tears in my eyes, of what my relative did. I also have learned it did happen in my mother's house when she was trying to protect me from the men in the streets. I used to sit in my room a lot. The only one I could trust was God. I thought that if I told anybody, they would look at me crazy. I feel comfortable now because I know other woman have gone through the same. I used to feel sex was ugly and I was scared of having sex. I never had a desire.

I would always take time to talk to God and my daughter. I was so bitter inside, I didn't want to talk or be bothered. I did feel God didn't protect me. I know today the hurt and pain I have inside isn't that bad, because the Holy Spirit lives within me. I realized today that I must first go through all the channels to love again.

At times, I feel the "little child" feeling of hurts. I am dealing with the past, choosing to deal with the dark secrets. I'm bringing them to God. I know God knows all the hurt and pain of my life. I have a friend, a counselor and mother to tell all of the hurts.

I have been seeking God's love. I am now revealing all of my secrets. Today, I can tell the whole story to my sisters in Christ and they will believe me. I thank the Lord for allowing me to look at the past. One day I hope I can help others by telling the people how God helped me through all of my situations. All of these years, I kept the secret of my life. I am beginning to tell people, about my child molestation and my marriage being a waste, freely because before I felt like no one liked me unless I had something to give them.

I want to talk to my brother and husband to explain things to them. But I understand they are very bitter inside. I do wonder if I really will have an enjoyable sex life again. The Lord is filling me from my past.

I always wondered if my secrets would be found out. Would I be able to enjoy sex again? We didn't talk about sexual abuse. All of my memories were so painful with bitterness inside from child molestation. I thought I would be nothing for the rest of my life. I used alcohol and drugs just to face the day. I thought I needed to be punished; I didn't see the love I had from my family.

My relative denied the idea of what he had done to me, the molestation. I began living life out of destruction; I worked but I could not keep a job. I loved working; the drugs stopped me. I went into denial, because I trusted my relatives so much. I have learned my mind just shattered some. When another sister shared her testimony, she explained that she was molested as a child. I was feeling guilty at first of what my relatives had done to me. I thought God couldn't forgive me.

Today, by my trusting Christ as my Savior, I receive special grace. I know today that God accepted me though; I thought my family didn't. When I start believing God's promises for me, I discovered that the last of the evil spirits are still in me. I met different men, and I was so bound by drugs that my hurts went deeper. God has delivered me from child molestation and drugs. All I do is hope and pray that God delivers me from all the evil spirits.

I feel better I can share the hurt to different counselors. I use to feel so dirty inside I wanted to die. I do understand I have to forgive my relative and husband for everything I did. By my trusting in God, He keeps on breaking down walls of bitterness. I know today God has a listening ear. I must always allow the grace of God to work in my life as if I were a child. At times I feel the acceptance and love inside. I am very sensitive to my feeling for acceptance and rejection. When a sister in Christ or a counsel hugs me I feel real good inside. By my believing in God and receiving Him today I am a child of God. I have so much hatred inside of me for men I don't trust men. I do see my brother and all the other people who hurt me as human. I don't have feelings for taking vengeance into my own hands. I now know forgiveness is an act of my will. I want to forgive my relative and husband. Today I know it would stop my life if I don't, and my life still goes on.

I found out by asking the Lord to take the hatred out, it is beginning to work more. All I can do is pray that God will prepare and make his heart right.

To be incredulous about the evil of sexual abuse is to be naïve about what God says the human heart is capable of. At the same time, our God is a God of redemption and His word tells us that He is quite capable of reaching down in to a life that has been damaged by the evil of sexual abuse waiting to restore and redeem that life so it becomes a thing of beauty and brings glory to His name.

Violence and abuse, especially in the home, appears to be increasing. It is possible, of course that, we are only now beginning to recognize the widespread prevalence of a problem that has been with us for centuries.

Abuse is difficult to define, perhaps because the term covers so many types of physical and psychological maltreatment. Child abuse involves the "physical or mental injury, sexual abuse of exploitation, negligent treatment, or maltreatment of a child under the age of eighteen, by a person who is responsible for the child's welfare and under circumstances which indicate the child's health or welfare is harmed or threatened thereby." Sexual abuse may overlap with any of the above and includes exhibitionism, forced intercourse or other sexual behavior which the victim resists, or fondling the sex organs of a minor or other person who is naïve or powerless to resist.

Just as abuse is difficult to define, so is the amount of incidents difficult to measure. Many victims are reluctant to report abuse, especially when the abuser is a family member. Children often are unable to report abuse, and some people aren't even aware that the pain they experience is abuse.

Depending on the age, personality, sex, type of abuse and past experiences of the victim, the effects of abuse can influence people in a variety of ways. When compared with non-victims, for example, incest victims are more inclined to show inability to trust others, low self-esteem, conflicts over sexual identity, feelings of guilt or shame and isolation from others.

Post-sexual-abuse syndrome can be characterized by anxiety, sleep disturbances, anger, sexual dysfunction, substance addiction, and self-destructive tendencies. The adult victims of child abuse often become overweight, depressed, and chronically anxious.

Many had nightmares; almost all had problems with sex, and most had difficulties forming stable relationships. Some appeared to be intent on making themselves appear unattractive to others. Teenagers who had been abused or neglected, as children, are more likely than the non-abused to be involved in delinquent behavior and to commit violent crimes.

Finally, we should not forget the abuser. Often these people feel deep and lasting remorse, especially after their abusive behavior becomes public knowledge. Many are frightened, guilt-ridden, and confused, but they find little support or sympathy from others. Few attempt to understand abusers, and seem reluctant to realize that many abusers need help as much as their victims.

In the midst of grieving, relatives sometimes try to protect children from the realities and sadness of death. It should be remembered, however, that children also have a need to grieve and to understand as best they can.

To really understand death, children must be able to distinguish between themselves and others, between living and nonliving, between thought and reality, and between past, present, and future. Whether or not the child has this understanding, he or she must be helped to comprehend the finality of death, to express emotion, and to ask questions. It is important to reassure children (repeatedly by words and actions) that they are loved and will be cared for. Children often interpret death, especially the death of a parent, as a form of rejection.

The Missing Pieces

"My life has been enriched by the remarkable hope, trust, and faith that God will make a way. I have learned that my father was an alcoholic and I was very hurt from this issue-I started punishing myself for not being a mother, sister or daughter. I had a lot of bitterness and hurt inside of me, from childhood molestation. Lately, I am able to talk to my counselor about the problems in my life.

Today, I can say, I have given myself to Christ and that's my biggest commitment. I can remember saying and I still say the Lord had mercy on my soul. When I gave this issue to God and prayed, I felt much better.

I didn't realize my trust in the Lord was so sacred. I must always remember, God answers prayers. Today, I know it is God's will to let things happen. I just hope and pray if it's the will of the Lord to see him again. This is one of the missing pieces of my life."

"And without faith it is impossible to please God, because anyone who comes to him must believe that he exists and that he rewards those who earnestly seek him" Hebrews 11:6 (NIV).

Acknowledging grief over the loss of a child through adoption, and dealing with feelings of shame and guilt are important steps for parents who are placed voluntarily and for those who did not.

Birthmothers' relinquishment of experiences has affected their relationships with themselves and with the significant people in their lives. Through analysis, common themes of unresolved issues are identified. The results indicate that birthmothers still struggle with low self-esteem, reproduction and parenting issues, failed relationships and dreams of reuniting with her lost children. The findings suggest that the loss extends further than indicated and may encompass more issues such as alcoholism and physical and sexual abuse in the families of origin.

When a woman discovers she is pregnant, she naturally begins a process of life-altering change. If the pregnancy is unplanned, not only is the woman's life altered, but also the negative repercussions are great. These include dealing with the experience of loss and trauma, affecting the woman's relationship with herself, her family, her community, her school or work, her health, and her social as well as her spiritual life. She will eventually be forced to address the serious issues of her circumstances and to choose among potentially painful and difficult alternatives.

One of the traditionally accepted alternatives for an unwanted pregnancy is adoption. Adoption has a profound and permanent effect on the lives of all members of the adoption triad: the birthparents, the adoptee, and the adoptive parents. Most of their issues have to do with loss that is often denied or suppressed. Frequently adoption issues go untreated in the therapy room because many therapists are unaware of the far-reaching impact it has made on clients who are part of the adoption triad.

Unfortunately, the failure to identify adoption as an important issue eliminates the possibility of addressing therapeutic issues resulting from adoption, thus maintaining the secrets and keeping hidden and unresolved the losses suffered. This omission increases the likelihood that the unhealed wounds and the behaviors that surround them will be passed on to the next generations, to perhaps repeat the cycle once again.

Our culture has not only failed to provide rituals, which support the birthmother in grieving the losses she suffers, it hasn't even given her permission to grieve. Thus, many women who have relinquished a child have suffered alone, feeling guilty, ashamed, and unworthy of consolation and healing.

Existing studies of the birthmother confirm overwhelmingly that there are long-enduring effects of having experienced the loss of a child to adoption. The post-adoption experience of the birthmothers determines that the unhealed loss manifests itself in areas of trouble, failed or multiple marriages, infertility, struggle with parenting, and low self-worth. The birthmother may experience emotional numbness, a sense of powerlessness and emptiness, and may suffer from low self-esteem. She can be wrought with feelings of guilt, shame, and anger, and may suffer from anxiety, depression, agoraphobia, eating disorders, or chemical dependency.

She may have an unconscious fear of sex and may experience discomfort being around children. If she has subsequent children, she may become either overprotective and possessive or perfectionistic and distant, feeling she is inadequate at being a mother. Whatever her circumstances, she has neither forgotten, nor stopped loving her child, and her grieving is a potentially life-long process. It has been an accepted practice to encourage the birthmother to bury the experience and quickly "get on with her life".

Existing information about how deeply the birthmother has been affected by the relinquishment of her child will help society become more aware about how to deal with adoption in the future. Since the literature falls short of providing suggestions for services for birthmothers who want to heal, the next step is to raise the consciousness among the mental health community about her needs and create services for her recovery.

For healing, the birthmother is to be assisted to free herself from the secrecy with which she has lived, to validate her feelings and express her denied emotions, to create rituals for grieving, to develop new relationships with supportive people, to participate in support groups with other birthmothers, and, if she feels the need after her healing has begun, to search for her child.

Faith has always been the mark of God's servants, from the beginning of the world. Where the regenerating Spirit of God plants the principle, it will cause the truth to be received of the things that are the object of our hope, the object of our faith. It is a firm persuasion and expectation, that God will perform all He has promised to us. This persuasion gives the soul to enjoy those things now.

Faith proves to the mind, the reality of things that cannot be seen by the bodily eye. It is a full approval of all God has revealed, as holy, just, and good. This view of faith is explained by many examples of persons in former times, which obtained a good report, or an honorable character in the word of God. Faith was the principle of their holy obedience, remarkable services, and patient sufferings.

Men may shut up their compassion; yet, with God we shall find mercy. This is great comfort to all believers, plainly to be seen, and not to be taken away. God does all wisely and well; but what or how He does things, we know not until it is time. God's loving-kindness is precious to them that put themselves under His protection. God works by His Spirit filling their souls with joy and peace. May we know, and love, and uprightly serve the Lord; then no proud enemy, on earth or from hell, shall separate us from His love. Faith calleth things that are not, as though they were. It carries us forward with hope.

God made all human life legitimate, regardless of the circumstances surrounding the conception.

Why I Feel I Am Ready To Move On To The Second Phase Program?

"When I first came to Teen Challenge, I did not have any hope. Now I can face tomorrow without fear and I know the right and wrong things of life. I didn't have any responsibilities and I did not want any responsibilities. I now have a desire to serve God. What I mean by this is I want to help new sisters by giving them encouraging words of love and understanding. Because today I have the strength God has given to me to take on responsibilities. Today I have a humble heart and attitude to listen to my authorities when I am told to do something. I have a reverent attitude, because I respect my authorities and my sisters. I have a willing attitude and heart to be like Jesus. Today I can now say there's no separation between God and I. I also have a desire to share what God has done in my life to other people. Also, to minister to groups of people, what

God have done in my life. This is the biggest commitment in my life. I feel very special inside and I want to show my gratitude.

Since being at Teen Challenge, my desire for New York is different. I would like to live in New York; there are so many different opportunities to further my education. The ways of communication in New York is very simple. Subways and buses are easy to catch; also, they run very frequently. The diverse culture satisfies the new desire to meet different people in their walk with Christ.

Since I suffer with HIV, the benefits are great with a high rate of children who have HIV. I want to give my service to them. I want to be able to assist in restoring souls."

Waiting On God

"I know today my faith is on the right track. I know today God is doing a complete work in my life. I have learned that the ability for waiting on God is His grace cultivated within me.

When I pray during the day, I'm showing my expression of my personal relationship with God. I do believe God hears my cries and answers all of my prayers.

I'm opening my heart to God and I'm seeking a fellowship with God. The more I yield to God, the more blessings are coming to me. I'm very patient in the Lord and I'm resting on His promises. I know today, I trust in the Lord with all of my heart and soul. God is comforting my heart of a lot of aches and pains. By the grace of God and His faith, I'm able to receive His precious glory. I have learned, God gives me the strength to renew my mind, run and not get weary, walk and not be faint. Through exercising my faith, I get my strength. Today, I know God gives me the strength to renew my mind-educate myself and He satisfies my soul. I have learned, that God is doing a perfect redemption in my soul.

God is revealing Christ in me through the Holy Spirit. Also, I have learned by being myself, by letting God have His way, He's revealing Christ in me through the Holy Spirit. I know today, that the full revelation of Christ is the divine communication of Himself. Today, I know God is filling all of my promises and His promises lives within me. He's restoring my soul. He's giving me new life, and He's giving me the Fruit of the Spirit. I must continue to just keep on waiting on God. Today, I know the Holy Spirit, lives in me."

"But they that wait upon the LORD shall renew their strength; they shall mount up with wings as eagles; they shall run, and not be weary; and they shall walk, and not faint."

Isaiah 40:31 (KJV)

We should wait on God, through our deliverance, trials and tribulations of building a relationship with Him. Those who think they can do it on their own end up obsessed with measuring their own moral muscle but never get around to exercising it in real life. Those who trust God's action in them find that God's Spirit is in them is alive God!

Obsession with self in these matters is a dead end; attention to God leads us out into the open, into a spacious, free life. Focusing on the self is the opposite of focusing on God. Anyone completely absorbed in self ignores God, ends up thinking more about self than God. That person ignores who God is and what He is doing. It stands to reason, God raised Jesus from the dead, He'll do the same thing in us that He did in Jesus, bringing us alive to himself.

When God lives and breathes in us, we are delivered from that dead life. We are enlarged in the waiting. We, of course, don't see what is enlarging us. But the longer we wait, the larger we become, and the more joyful our expectancy.

Meanwhile, the moment we get tired in the waiting, God's Spirit is right alongside helping us along. We should let God do the work completely as it pleases Him. Waiting becomes then the only way to the experience of a full salvation, the knowledge of God as our salvation. Let us strive to see what the elements are that make up this most blessed and needful waiting on God, it may help us to discover the reason why this grace is cultivated.

Waiting on God is the nature of man and the nature of God. God formed man, to be a vessel in which He could show forth his power and goodness. It is God, alone who began the work of redemption.

Renewing Of the Mind

"Three months ago I thought it was the end of my life but God restored it. When I was a sinner I didn't accept things that God provided. I used to have it all-clothes, money, cars, good education, husband and family. But it became greed for abundance, never satisfied. Since I have been saved, my problems and struggles have disappeared somewhat. I know God wants to do His work and His good pleasure in me. The old has gone and the new has come. Today, I know I am a living sacrifice, holy and pleasing to him. A living sacrifice causes a transformation of my human personality. God's will is what I want for my life. Today, I know God's way is opposite of my way.

Through using drugs at sixteen years old, I stopped growing emotionally, psychologically. Satan had access to my mind totally. I have learned today my mind is a battlefield, a spiritual warfare between God and Satan. I now know my mind determines my words and actions. If I think of fearful thoughts, I will live in fear.

I should love neighbors as I love myself. I know today, if I stop meditating on the Lord, I will do opposite of a godly way. I know today, God can meet all of my needs and desires. God wants my mind to be sensitive to the Holy Spirit. I know today my mind is being renewed, because I feel the presence of the Lord within me."

"I beseech you therefore, brethren, by the mercies of God, that you present your bodies a living sacrifice, holy, acceptable to God, which is your reasonable service. And do not be conformed to this world, but be transformed by the renewing of your mind, that you may prove what is that good and acceptable and perfect will of God" Romans 12:1&2 (KJV).

According to the Bible, the mind is unusual in that it constitutes a battlefield where Satan and his evil spirits contend against the truth and hence against the believer. Scripture explains that before regeneration "the god of this world had blinded the minds of the unbelievers, to keep them from seeing the light of the gospel of the glory of Christ, who is the likeness of God" (2 Corinthians 4:4). Satan holds on to man's mind by making it blind: Satan has covered the eyes of man's mind.

When firmly held by Satan, the mind of man becomes "hardened;" man follows the desires of body and mind as "children of wrath" and so "is estranged and hostile in mind" because "the mind that is set on the flesh is hostile to God" (2 Corinthians 3:14; Ephesians 2:3; Colossians 1:21; Romans 8:7). We can see clearly how the powers of darkness are especially related to man's mind, how it is peculiarly susceptible to Satan's assault. With respect to man's will, emotion and body, the powers of evil are helpless to do anything directly unless they first have gained some ground therein. But with man's mind, they can work freely without initially persuading man or securing his invitation.

Man's mind is especially related to Satan. If we were to peruse the scriptures carefully and to observe the experiences of the saints, we would discover that all communications between human and satanic forces occur in thought. Take, for instance, Satan's temptation. Every temptation, which entices man, is presented to his mind. It is true that Satan often uses the flesh to secure the consent of man; yet in each instance of enticement, the enemy creates some kind of thought by which to induce the man. We cannot separate temptation and thought.

All temptations are offered us in the form of thoughts. Man in his mind is at enmity with God; therefore, God must alter man's mind if He would impart life to him. Because it has been so united with the devil, it is vital for man to receive a new heart. But even following repentance, the believer's mind is not liberated totally from the touch of Satan. Satan did not assail Eve's heart first but rather her head. Similarly today, evil spirits first attack our head not heart, in order to have us corrupted from the simplicity and purity, which is towards Christ.

It is possible for a child of God to have a new life and a new heart but be without a new head. With too many saints, the mind, though their heart is new, is still quite old. Their heart is full of love whereas their head is totally lacking in perception. Often the intents of heart are utterly pure and yet the thoughts in the head are confused. The mind lacks the most single element of all, which is spiritual insight. Christians ought to realize that even ones who maintain the most intimate fellowship with God may nevertheless unknowingly have accepted Satan's suggestions in his mind, which consequently precipitate errors in his conduct, words and viewpoints.

God wishes to restore our thought life to the excellent state it had when He created it so that we may not only glorify God in our walk but may glorify Him in our thinking as well. The Lord's people need to know that if they want to live a full life their mind must be renewed. One of the reasons why the Kingdom of God lacks workers today is because too many cannot undertake anything with their head. They neglect to seek its renewal after they are saved permitting their work to be obstructed. We must "be transformed by the renewal of our mind."

God desires not only a change in the mind of His children at the time of conversion; He desires also a mind that is totally renewed, which is transparent as crystal. Once knowing the teaching of Romans 6 many Christians see themselves as having already been freed from their carnal mind. What they do not appreciate is that the cross must operate minutely in every area of the man. "Consider yourselves dead to sin" must be followed by "let not sin therefore reign in you mortal bodies" Romans 6:11-12.

Following the change of mentality there must be the bringing of "every thought captive to obey Christ" (2 Corinthians 10:5). The mind must be renewed, completely, since any residue of its carnality is hostile to God.

For us to have our intellects renewed, we must draw near to the cross. We know that our old man has been crucified with the mind (Romans 6:6), which brings the cross into view as the instrument for its renewal. The salvation, which God imparts through the cross, includes not only a new life but the renewal of every function of our soul as well. The salvation, which is rooted deeply in our being, must be "worked out."

Upon recognizing the staleness of his mind and being willing to put it off by the cross, the Christian now should practice denying all carnal thoughts daily. The believer in addition should assail the lies of the evil spirits. Every suggestion from the enemy must be met resolutely with the truth of the Bible. Answer doubt with the texts of faith; respond to despair with words of hope; reply to fear with words of peace. If he does not know the appropriate verse, let him pray for direction; if he recognizes that something is from his foes, then he can say to them, "This is your lie, I will not accept it." Victory is obtained by wielding the Sword of the Spirit.

"I will put my laws into their minds," declares God (Hebrews 8:10). We should read and memorize more of the Word of God, unless we are unable to find it at the moment of urgent need. If we diligently read the Bible God will fill every thought of ours with His laws.

The Christian continually ought to ask God to purify his mental life and keep it fresh, pray that you may only think of Him but in addition think rightly. Ask God to keep you away from your old pattern of thinking.

Chapter Three

Developing the Mind of Christ

"The man without the Spirit does not accept the things that come from the Spirit of God, for they are foolishness to him, and he cannot understand them, because they are spiritually discerned" 1 Corinthians 2:14 (KJV).

The natural man, the wise man of the world, receives not the things of the Spirit of God. The pride of carnal reasoning is really as much opposed to spirituality, as the basis of sensuality. The sanctified mind discerns the real beauties of holiness, but the power of discerning and judging about common and natural things is not lost.

But the carnal man is a stranger to the principles, and pleasures, and actions of the Divine life. The spiritual man only, is the person to whom God gives the knowledge of His will. How little have any known of the mind of God by natural power!

In the Scriptures, the mind of Christ, and the mind of God in Christ, are fully made known to us. It is the great privilege of Christians, that they have the mind of Christ revealed to them by his Spirit. They experience his sanctifying power in their hearts, and bring forth good fruits in their lives.

Developing The Roots Of Christian Characters

"I have a lot of pride in myself. I want to know, how I can be perfect in the sight of God. I have learned that God wants me to keep his Ten Commandments holy. In doing this, I must remember to keep His commandment through my Spirit. I have the desire to be like Jesus.

At times, I don't feel like I should apologize to a sister when she offends me. I'm praying to the Lord to make me humble and to be what He wants me to be. I'm learning to live right and to hate sin. Through God's grace, I have the freedom not to sin.

Also, through the Holy Spirit, I can see a lot of bad areas in my life. I'm praying for the Lord to build my faith up. For today, I know there's nothing impossible with God.

I'm learning to stand firm with some of the sisters. I know there's a lot of flesh left within me. Through, God's Words and of the Holy Spirit, I can live a righteous life. I always pray for endurance and the Fruit of the Spirit. God wants to deal with me in becoming a good Christian."

"But the fruit of the Spirit is love, joy, peace, patience, kindness, goodness, faithfulness, gentleness and self-control. Against such things there is no law."

Galatians 5:22&23 (NIV)

The Fruit of the Spirit is the moral character developed by the power of the Spirit. The nine character qualities are a unity, a perfectly formed Christ like character. These character qualities are not a new list of laws or moral codes that must be kept; they are the result of living and being led by the Spirit. The Spirit will produce those moral qualities that God requires.

Love is the focus of the entire ethical appeal: "serve one another in love". Love fulfills the law; love is the expression of faith. Love is demonstrated in a tangible way in the sacrificial love of Christ and the service of Christians. All the other moral qualities in the list define and flow from love. Joy is the result of healthy relationships. When relationships fall apart because of broken commitments, there is a loss of joy. When there is conflict and bitterness, there is no joy. But the first result of true love in relationships is the renewal of joy. Peace is also the result of relationships built by loving service. Instead of "hatred, discord, dissensions, factions" there is harmony and order in relationships.

Patience is the opposite of "fits of rage" or short temper. It is the quality of staying with people even when constantly wronged and irritated by them. Kindness and goodness are joined with patience to teach that a sweet disposition and doing good toward people is the way to stay with them in love.

Faithfulness is the quality of keeping commitments in relationships. Only the Spirit can produce the quality of loyalty no matter the cost. Gentleness is the opposite of "selfish ambition". Gentle people are not "conceited, provoking and envying each other". Gentleness is an expression of humility, considering the needs and hurts of others before one's personal goals. Self-control is the opposite of self-indulgence.

Those who are Spirit-led will not indulge the sinful nature. They do not use other people to gratify their own appetites. They have the strength to say no to themselves, to the desires of their sinful nature. The Spirit-led life is not a life against the law; it is a life that fulfills the law. The way to the fulfillment of the law is not to live under the law like slaves, but to live by the Spirit as children of God. The only treatment for the cancer of pride is: we must crucify the pride of sinful nature and be led by the Spirit, who alone has the power to overthrow the dictatorship of pride.

Adventures In Prayer

"The Holy Spirit is digging deep of the hatred, inside of me. I asked Him to take the hurting pain out of me. I must remember and believe to trust in the Lord, lean not to my own understanding. I'm learning to trust the counselors more. Today, I know that Christ lives within me. By the grace of God, with the help of one counselor in particular, I'm learning to trust God.

Since I came to Teen Challenge, God is providing a way for me through my sister for the things that Teen Challenge does not do. My sister use to see how dead I looked on the outside. I prayed for restoration; God is restoring my soul and He's also healing my body. By my praying to the Lord to help, He reveals my past and cleans out the evil spirits. I know Jesus cares, because it's important to me to let him do the work.

I know today, God does release evil spirits through the Holy Spirit. God is teaching me the warfare is not against flesh and blood but against the wicked spirits that rule the darkness of this world. "Our fight is not with people. It is against the leaders and the powers and the spirits of darkness in this world. It is against the demon world that works in the heavens" (Ephesians 6:12 (NLV). I thought I would never be able to release the bitterness, aches and pain I had on the inside. I' m praying to the Lord about these problems and He keeps on making a way for me. By trusting God, I do have the victory. The Lord waited for me, He kept his angels over me. He set me free from drugs. My drug addiction lasted twenty-three years. I do understand God does answer prayers.

I just don't pray on Sundays, but all day Sunday (Mark 1:35). I talk to God when I'm getting ready for church, later when I go back to rest. Blessed at a service; I spend time with God in prayer. I pray daily; my total dependence is on Him. Even if is a couple of minutes out of each hour, I pray.

Lately when praying for different sisters, I have been asking God to bless them and their loved ones with his diving power. I know today God's blessing me in so many ways, I feel so anointed inside. Today I know I'm filled with the Holy Spirit.

Today, I know God has a plan for me, to be prosperous and successful. I want to be a servant of God to minister to people, what God has done in my life. I'm learning to become a leader and not a follower. All I have to remember is to be a living sacrifice holy, pleasing to God. God is fulfilling, all of His promises. My goal is to be a Christian Drug Counselor and Restoration Minister."

"Trust in the LORD with all your heart and lean not on your own understanding; in all your ways acknowledge him, and he will make your paths straight" Proverbs 3:5 (NIV).

When we have an important decision to make, we sometimes feel that we can't trust anyone-not even God. But God knows what is best for us. He is a better judge of what we want than even we are!

We must trust Him completely in every choice we make. This does not mean we cannot study the options and make intelligent decisions, or that we should have no confidence in our ability. It means, however, that we must not be wise in our own eyes.

We should always be willing to listen to and be corrected by others. Bring your decisions to God in prayer; use the Bible as your guide; and then do what is right.

Experiencing God through Prayer

"I know today when I go through trials, tribulations; I should just keep on persevering. I have asked the Lord to take away the desire of men, money and clothes. I know today, God has chosen me to turn away from my wicked ways and also away from this evil world. I'm learning to cast all of my problems on the Lord and to keep my eyes on Jesus.

Today I know I have eternal life in Christ Jesus. As long as I allow the Holy Spirit to work in me, I will continuously grow as a new creation. I love the Lord with all of my heart soul and my mind. I pray daily for the Lord to draw me closer to Him. I definitely know God is in the operating business. I know today I want to be strong in the Lord. One day I will be a living sacrifice, holy and pleasing unto Him. I will be a godly Christian woman one day."

"Pray continually" 1 Thessalonians 5:17 (NIV).

Through daily prayer, you can be drawn closer to God and love Him more. "As the deer pants for water, so I long for you, O God. I thirst for God, the living God" (Psalm 42:1-2 LAB).

As the life of a deer depends upon water, our lives depend upon God. Those who seek Him and long to understand Him find never-ending life. Feeling a separation from God, do not rest until the relationship with God has been restored because your life depends on it.

God stands ready to hear us, to forgive our sins, and to restore our relationship to Him. He is ready to forgive us and restore us to fellowship with Him. Dedicate your body as the temple of God, set yourself apart exclusively for His purpose-to worship God through prayer.

The Process To Spiritual Growth

1. How God Uses Circumstances. *"You can be transformed into the character of Christ.*

In order to draw closer to God, one must be transformed into a new creation. The lifestyle I lived for so long was so ugly inside. I know today God has begun a good work in my life because I don't like the spirit of pride. For the last couple of months God has put different sisters in my life to identify pride.

I have learned that I want to be one of God's servants. I know today God is inside of me and I want to be transformed into a new creation. I have learned I used to brag about myself pertaining to my past life and my present life. Yes, different sisters started to give me the cold shoulders. Also, I definitely did not like criticism. I wanted God to take this feeling out of me. I also have learned I do have a spirit of jealousy and selfishness inside of me.

At one time, I thought it was wrong to be angry or discouraged as a Christian. I'm going to allow the Holy Spirit, which lives within me to work for I don't want anything to come between God and I."

2. God's Pressure Cooker. *"I must give up pride to serve God in a mighty way. I have learned, that my heart can be deceitful in thinking different situations are all right. I have learned, I was self-confident in myself; I thought I had everything in life. Now today I have nothing. I had bragged on my self tremendously. All of my life, I was self-sufficient. Today, I need God in my life because I can't do anything by myself. I want so bad to die to self and I'm learning to pick up my cross daily. I lost my integrity many years ago. All I wanted to do was give up. For I thank God He's restoring my life. God is also providing me with the love I never had.*

God is also giving me peace within myself today. Also, I have learned that I was put in different situations to see pride. God is also bringing my family back together again. Yesterday, it had gotten to the point I wanted to scream. Today, I can do all things through God who strengthens me."

3. The Process Of Bearing Fruit. *"When I first came to Teen Challenge, I did not have hope, peace, joy, love any type of godly character at all. All I could do was just keep on praying for the Holy Spirit to help me. I always take time to read the Word and apply the scriptures to my life. I always pray for the Holy Spirit to give me the desire to learn His ways and words. I did not have the memory to think about anything. I was dead inside. I pray daily that the Holy Spirit will pour His love all over me. From God's love I am able to share love for others.*

Yes, I'm able to distinguish wrong from right. I have a feeling of drawing closer to God. When I was praying for pride, selfishness and jealousy, I began to feel a change. I'm learning to live righteous for I feel the truth will set me free. I do not complain or grumble anymore for I know there is a reason for every rule in Teen Challenge. I cannot live any other way but to live righteously. My plans are to stay at Teen Challenge, to let the Lord complete the work He has begun in me."

Passion And Purity

"Through God's grace, I can feel His presence all around me. God is teaching me, I'm special in His sight. God is teaching me that the inner beauty of myself is most important.

God's strength is my joy today. God is preparing me to be Jesus Christ's bride. Jesus is the first love in my life. God's love and compassion is unconditional for me always. Through God's grace the fruit of the Spirit is blossoming in me. God's love, joy and peace feel so good inside of me. My love for the Lord is very intimate. God has given me the strength to put all of my hope in Christ Jesus today.

God has given me the ears to listen to the Holy Spirit. God has given me the desire to not separate myself from Him. I'm going to continue to stand firm and seek the Lord. The love of the Lord feels so good."

Character Qualities

1. Patience. "We can rejoice, too when we run into problems and trials for we know that they are good for us, they help us learn to be patient. And patience develop strength of character in us and help us learn to trust God more each time we use it until, finally our hope and faith are strong and steady" Romans 5:3&4 (TLB).

"Patience is the opposite quality of restlessness. It is learning how to wait to fulfill personal goals. It increases the time you can wait between achievement and reward. It is learning to accept difficult situations from God without giving Him a deadline to remove them."

2. Self-control. "Those who belong to Christ have nailed their natural evil desires to His cross and crucified them there. If we are living now by the Holy Spirit's power, let us follow the Holy Spirit's leading in every part of our lives" Galatians 5:24&25 (TLB).

"Self-control is the opposite quality of self-indulgence. It is learning to quickly identify and obey the initial promptings of the Holy Spirit. It is bringing thoughts, words and actions under the control of the Holy Spirit."

3. Meekness. "My Christian brothers, you know everyone should listen much and speak little. He should be slow to become angry. A man's anger does not allow him to be right with God" James 1:19&20 (NLT).

"Meekness is the opposite quality of anger. It is learning how to yield rights and possessions to God. It is responding properly when others violate personal rights. It is learning to earn the right to be heard rather than demanding a hearing."

4. Sensitivity. "When others are happy, be happy with them. If they are sad share in their sorrows" Romans 12:15 (TLB).

"Sensitivity is the opposite quality of callousness. It is exercising the senses to perceive the true spirit and emotions of those around me. It is being alert to the promptings of the Holy Spirit. Sensitivity is avoiding danger by sensing wrong motives in others; knowing how to give the right words at the right time."

5. Humility. "If someone mistreats you because you are a Christian, don't curse him, pray that God will bless him" Romans 12:14 (TLB). "But he gives us more and more strength to stand against all such evil longings. As the Scripture says: God gives strength to the humble, but sets himself against the proud and the haughty" James 4:6 (TLB).

"Humility is the opposite quality of pride. It is recognizing my total inability to accomplish anything for God apart from His grace. It understands how deceitful the heart is. It the ability to be quick to direct praises to God and others, to distinguish between flattery and praise."

6. Tolerance. "Then make me truly happy by loving each other and agreeing whole heartedly with each other, working together with one heart and mind and purpose" Philippians 2:2 (TLB).

"Tolerance is the opposite quality of prejudice. It is learning how to respond to the immaturity of others without accepting their standard of immaturity."

7. Security. "But you shouldn't be so concerned about perishable things like food. No, spend your energy seeking the eternal life that I, the Messiah, can give you. For God the Father has sent me for this very purpose" John 6:27 (TLB). "Trust in the Lord with all your heart. Never rely on what you think you know. Remember the Lord in everything you do, and He will show you the right way" Proverbs 3:5&6 (GNB).

"Security is the opposite quality of anxiety. It is learning to build affections around the person of Christ and His eternal Word. It is learning to appreciate temporal possessions without making them the focus of your delight."

8. Loyalty. "And here is how to measure it—the greatest love is shown when a person lays down his life for his friends" John 15:13 (TLB).

"Loyalty is the opposite of unfaithfulness. It is adopting as your own wishes and goals of those you are serving. It is learning to stand by those you are serving when conflicting pressures increase."

9. Dependability. "He despises those whom God rejects, but honor those who obey the Lord. He always does what he promises, no matter how much it may cost" Psalm 15:4 (GNB).

"Dependability is the opposite quality of inconsistency. It is learning to be true to your word even when it is difficult to carry out what you promised to do. It is lifting pressure from those you serve by consistently fulfilling the project they assign to you."

10. Virtue. "Finally, brothers, whatever is true, whatever is noble, whatever is right, whatever is pure, whatever is lovely, whatever is admirable—if anything is excellent or praiseworthy—think about such things" Philippians 4:8 (NIV).

"Virtue is the opposite quality of vice. It is conformity to godly morality. It is exemplifying moral excellence and righteousness".

11. Discretion. "A prudent man foresee the difficulties ahead and prepares for them; the simpleton goes blindly on and suffers the consequences" Proverbs 22:3 (TLB).

"Discretion is the opposite quality of simple-mindedness. It is learning how to respond in difficult situations with the wisdom and character of Christ. It is the knowledge of that which is appropriate or inappropriate. Discretion is seeing the consequences of words and actions further down the road."

12. Love. "And so I am giving a new commandment to you now-love each other just as much as I love you. Your strong love for each other will prove to the world that you are my disciples." John 13:34&35 (NLT)

"Love is the opposite quality of selfishness. It is learning how to give to the basic needs of others without motive for a personal reward."

13. Responsibility. "While I am talking with you there, I will give them some of your authority, so they can share responsibility for my people. You will no longer have to care for them by yourself." Numbers 11:17 (CEV)

"Responsibility is the opposite quality exemption. It is learning to make the right choices and living with the consequences. It is a state of being accountable and/or reliable involving duties."

14. Fairness. "Treat others as you want them to treat you" Luke 6:31 (TLB).

"Fairness is the opposite quality of partiality. It is learning to look at a situation through the eyes of each one involved in it. It is making proper rewards to those who helped you accomplish your goals. It is learning to gather all of the facts before making a conclusion."

15. Decisiveness. "On with it, then, finish the job. Be as eager to finish it as you were to plan it, and do it with what you now have" 2 Corinthians 8:11 (GNB).

"Decisiveness is the opposite quality of double mindedness. It is learning to finalize difficult decisions based on God's will and way. It is refusing to reconsider decisions, which we know are right. It is making present commitments to avoid future failures."

Chapter Four

Being Rooted and Established in God

The end of every believer's process of redemption is to be rooted and established in God warranting God's favor, when suffering, to maintain the level of faith. Through prayer and supplication, one can obtain this goal.

"Now if we died with Christ, we believe that we will also live with him. For we know that since Christ was raised from the dead, he cannot die again; death no longer has mastery over him. The death he died, he died to sin once for all; but the life he lives, he lives to God" Romans 6:8-10 (NIV).

"I have been crucified with Christ and I no longer live, but Christ lives in me. The life I live in the body, I live by faith

in the Son of God, who loved me and gave himself for me" Galatians 2:20 (NIV).

The Work Of The Cross

1. Deliverance From The Old Creation.

"God gives more and more of an understanding of how I was delivered from the Kingdom of Darkness and that I'm a new creation in Christ Jesus. God is teaching me that I'm now a child of God and I now live in the Kingdom of God. Through the Holy Spirit and God's divine power the veil has been removed from my eyes. God is teaching me that by His grace I'm alive in Christ Jesus. God has given me the hunger and thirst for righteousness. He has filled my cup with His love, joy and peace.

God is teaching me to continually seek Him and pray in the Spirit. He is also teaching me that I must fast to get closer to Him. God has given me a grateful heart. God has given me a clear vision to see how beautiful the world looks. God has given me a desire to follow Him."

You must carry the cross to become resurrected from the dead but alive in Christ Jesus. You must get your heart right with God by confessing your sins and believing Jesus is our Mediator.

2. Reigning In Life With Christ

"I'm learning that God will make me the head of the nation and not the tail. Thereby, God is teaching me to live by His power. God is teaching me as long as I reign in His life, nothing can defeat me; I should continue to become totally effected by the cross. God is teaching me how to embrace the cross and then the cross will become my throne.

God has given all Christians the title of King. God is teaching me that Satan comes to steal, kill and destroy all of God's children. God will provide me with all of His riches and glories through Christ Jesus. God is teaching me that Jesus is the King of Kings, the Lord of Lords and He reigns all over the heaven and earth. I'm happy to know that Jesus is seated at the right hand side of God.

God has taught me I'm more than a conqueror through Christ Jesus. He is also teaching me to go out and proclaim the gospel, to win souls for Christ."

Christians have dominion over the fish in the sea and everything creeping on the earth. We as Christians have access to heaven. We can live a victorious life through Christ Jesus.

3. Deliverance From The Self-Life

"I have the authority to walk in the Spirit and not the lust of the flesh. God is teaching me that I must put on the Armor of God and pray in the Spirit daily. These weapons are to fight off principalities. God is teaching me that a carnal sin separates Him from me. To God Be The Glory that I have given my heart to Christ. God is teaching me I have a choice to live holy. I realize that every time I let my flesh get the best of me, I feel ugly. God is giving me an understanding that there is no condemnation in Christ Jesus when I fall short of the glory of God.

God is teaching me that His strength and grace will carry me through. That I have been crucified with Christ and I no longer live but Christ lives in me. The life I live in the body, I live by faith through the Son of God who loved me and gave himself for me. God is teaching me not to give the devil a foothold; if I do, I become angry. My flesh is my worst enemy. I should always seek the Lord daily, thank God more; His grace is sufficient today."

Christians are always blaming Satan when they sin against God. Christians have the authority not to feed the desires of the flesh, through the power of the Holy Spirit.

4. Deliverance From The Work Of The Devil

"Money and clothes are weak areas of my flesh. God is teaching me that I can continue to be set free of sin through His grace. God is teaching me that the full armor can help me fight in spiritual warfare. He is teaching me to pray in the Spirit. God is teaching me that He does not owe me anything, but I owe Him my life. God is increasing my faith every day through prayer. He is also letting me know that there will be trials and tribulations, but He promises never to leave me nor forsake me. God is teaching me Satan will attack me saying, I will always be a failure, but I know God's divine power is greater.

He also opened my eyes that the Blood of the Lamb is more powerful than Satan. God is teaching me that the one who is in me is greater than the one who is in the world!"

Jesus Christ's death on the cross-paid the price for our sins. Through God's abundant grace and righteousness, He will reign in our lives through His strength and not ours.

5. Deliverance From The Power Of Sin

"I am learning that the power of sin will keep me frustrated. God blessed me with His love, joy and peace when I was disciplined for gossiping. The power of sin will keep me from entering in the Kingdom of God. God is teaching me through His grace, I will continue to walk in newness of life.

God is teaching me that the old Phyllis is gone, that I'm a child of God. I have been crucified with Christ. He is also teaching me to continue to nail my natural evil desires to the cross. Through His strength, grace and power I am now dead to sin, but alive in Christ Jesus. God is always reminding me, this is the day He has made, to rejoice and be glad in it. The power of God can break bondages of sin. My spiritual ears are listening."

The blood of Jesus saves us from sin. Thereby, the wages of sin is death but the gift of God is eternal life. We as Christians are born with a sinful nature but we do have the victory through Jesus Christ.

Ordering Your Private World

"God has given me to have a private world with Him. God has given me the assurance, that I am drawing closer to Him. God has blessed me with a gift called faith and He is teaching me to exercise it. God has taught me not to draw attention to myself, but to focus on Him. He has given me wisdom to keep a planner, and a journal. God has taught me that I must continue to discipline myself by praying and reading the Word daily. God has taught me to take my time and to ask questions before I make a decision. God is teaching me to do everything at a pace, to totally depend on Him, to make my own decisions and to use the sound mind He has given me.

Through reading the Word, the Holy Spirit is renewing my mind. God is teaching me meditation demands a certain amount of imagination. God has taught me I can live a life of peace, a life of serenity and confidence through His strength. Before I gave my life to Christ, I was totally depended on others."

Successful Christians have a choice to live in a private world with Jesus Christ. The entire treatment of an order of private world is based on the principle of Christ, who enters our lives upon personal invitation and commitment.

I Have Grown In Christ

"Yes, I have grown in Christ. God has given me the victory through Him. He has given me a desire to have a private world with Him. God has given me wisdom that I know today (Jas 1:5). I must continue to discipline myself by praying and reading the Word daily (2 Tim. 2:15)

and to be still before Him in His presence. The more I read His Word, the more my faith will increase in Him.

I will continue to take my time and ask questions before I make decisions. I have learned how to keep a prayer journal and a daily planner. Meditation is reading a scripture and then using an imaginary mind (Josh. 1:8).

God has given me a heart to be loyal to Him. He has given me a desire to follow Him wherever He wants me to go. God has given me a grateful heart to thank Him daily for finding favor in me and to live by faith and not by sight (2 Cor. 5:7). The desire God has fulfilled in my heart (Ps. 37:4) is to forget about the past and to press toward the mark (Phil. 3:14).

He is raising me up to be a godly woman (Prov. 31). When I first came to Teen Challenge I talked like a child and I acted like a child, but, to God be the glory, I am a grown woman. He has raised me up to be a woman who is not ashamed of the Gospel of Jesus Christ (Rom 1:16).

He has taught me to live a clean innocent life as a child of God. I have learned grumbling and complaining are not pleasing in God's sight. I know better than to grumble or complain because it grieves the Holy Spirit.

God has totally won my trust in Him as being the Great I AM Who I Am in my life. The conviction of the Holy Spirit causes me to face Him. I know within my heart I never have to worry about what other people say about me. He has given me a desire in my heart so that I can say "Abba Father".

He has taught me to read the Word and how to apply the Word to my life, so I can resist the devil. I know today I will break the generational curse so that my daughter and grandson will have a good life. I must remember to rebuke Satan, when I feel abnormal-depressed by the onslaught of Satan. The power of God will help me fight my battles.

God's creation is awesome, He formed me, He created me, and I do not have to fear because He is right beside me. God continues to teach me to stand steady and not be afraid to suffer for the Lord.

God is teaching me to be confident in His love and His faithfulness. God is teaching me to respond with a Christ like attitude to all of His children. He keeps on reminding me that a gentle answer keeps away wrath. He giving me a strong love for Him and others to prove to the world I am a true disciple. I thank God for showing me when I point at another; it was to build up my own self-esteem. I must remember when trials and tribulations come my way, that God is with me and He uses them to make me more life Christ.

Yes, I had an inferiority complex that people would make fun of because I never smiled; my brothers use to call me Little Black Sheep of which time I used to want to give up. Today I have learned how to fight back with love. Yes, I went through emotional and sexual abuse battling at 0% percent, all because I wanted to be the daughter of great expectation. Without the help of God and my grandparents, I would have been put in an orphanage. Yes, I used to put others before myself for acceptance. But now, I know today I must continue to build a relationship with the Lord who made me.

I thank God, I still have a lot of things to work on; it is by the grace of God. For so many years, I was a "tramp" for Satan, now I want to be a "tramp" for the Lord. I used to think about death but now I think about life. The Lord has given me life. I do have compassion in my heart today. I do love singing to keep up courage. I know today God will restore all things for me. I know I'm trained to be kind. I know the Lord is sending me out to be a tramp for Him. I cried a many nights suffering; now, I thank the Lord for everything all day. I know today the Lord is preparing me to go to another phase of life with Him.

I know today I am here at this refuge for spiritual food, growth and healing from a broken heart."

Untwisting Twisted Relationships

"God has shown me that the many Christians who suffered from twisted relationships are very loving and caring on the inside. Yes, I often witnessed bad relationships; God has given me a clearer understanding for them not lasting. I had a twisted battle within myself. God will help me to build a true relationship with others through Jesus Christ. God has given me courage to expose the truth about my past relationships. God is teaching me I don't have to live up to others' expectations. God is teaching me to live up to His expectation. God is showing me I have been set free from rejection. The Holy Spirit is enabling me to look at life a brand new way. God spoke to me yesterday, He said He'd never let me be lonely. Today, I can say God has given me a desire to love others and I do know when I should love. God has given me the courage to be more open and honest about myself. God is definitely showing me I'm not perfect.

God has taught me to say no and not agree on everything a person says. He is showing me that some people will not like me as a new creation. Praise the Lord anyway. God is showing me that the best relationship I can ever have is being in love with Jesus. I see the areas of my life that God is working on. I know today, I must continue to build my relationship with the Lord first."

"Wherefore come out from among them, and be ye separate, saith the Lord, and touch not the unclean thing; and I will receive you" 2 Corinthians 6:17 (KJV).

God wants us to build a true relationship with Him first and then with other people. When we become Christians, we become part of God's family with fellow believers as our brothers and sisters. It is God who determines who the other family members are, not us. We are simply called to accept and love them.

A right relationship with God leads to right relationships with fellow believers. Although we will not always feel love toward all other believers, we must pursue peace, as we become more Christ like. Separation from the world involves more than keeping our distance from sinners; it means staying close to God. In this fallen world, there is no way to separate us totally from all effects of sin. Nevertheless, we are to resist the sin around us, not give up and give in.

Chapter Five

Restoring Broken Relationships

God's Call To Marriage

"When I got married to my husband I thought in my heart he was the right one for me. He was handsome, he had a lot of money and he was everything I had ever wanted. My relationship with him became very painful.

Every time he would say, "I love you" the words gave me security. I thought I could trust him because we were married and marriages were sacred. My marriage only lasted three months and the rest of the years he was in prison. For those three months together he would stay out all-night, indulging in cocaine and then come home saying "I love you, I'm sorry". I would forgive him. In my heart, I was saying I hated him, but out in the world we were taught love was having sex, so I continued fulfilling my marriage vows in every way for acceptance. He really didn't love me and I didn't really love him.

Again the drugs, I knew this was not love in our marriage, it was my first marriage and I failed as a woman. I began to live an insanely life using drugs all day long and all-night dealing with different men just to try to fill the void in my life. It had gotten to a point, I did not want to love anyone and I didn't' t want men to speak to be because I didn't trust them.

God wants me to have a successful marital relationship. God has filled the void in my heart of being lonely-I will have sexual desires, but I have the victory through Christ Jesus. God has given me a desire to cleave to Him for the rest of my life. He comes first and then my family. God has taught me marriage should not be considered, unless it is built in a relationship of growing love for each other. God has taught me communication plays a very important part with Him and my marriage. God has given me wisdom to make the right choices in my marriage. God has taught me how to speak gently. God has shown me His love never fails. God is the wise Counselor. I know today that wisdom comes from the Lord. God has taught me how to pray for guidance in my relationship with my husband."

"From the very first he made man and woman to be joined together permanently in marriage" Mark 10:6-7 (LAB).

God gave marriage as a gift to Adam and Eve. They were perfectly created for each other. Marriage was not just for convenience, nor was it brought about by any culture. It was instituted by God and has three basic aspects: (1) the man "leaves" his father and mother and in a public act, promises himself to his wife; (2) the man and woman are joined together by taking responsibility for each other's welfare and loving their mate above all others; (3) the two become "one person" or "one flesh" in the intimacy and commitment of sexual union which is reserved for marriage. Strong marriages today include all three of these aspects.

Marriage is a gift from God. It is valuable to accomplishing God's purpose-His creative way of providing companionship and populating the earth. His ideal is for marriages to be permanent, stay together. Christian married couples are to keep God first in their lives; real submission begins with Christ as Savior. The couples should work together as one; sin never unites, it always divides.

Dating Before Married

"My first relationship with a man was at the age of sixteen. As a child, I thought it was a woman's obligation to have a male companion to fall in love with him and to have a sexual relationship. I would always say I loved my mate, but I didn't know what true love was all about. Through my different relations with men, I became totally dependent on them. Even when I didn't want to be involved sexually, I felt intimidated, fearing they would find another woman. My joy and my self-worth were based on a man telling me He loved me. This type of love became a part of my life. My mind became so corrupt that if a man said he loved me, I would think he was lying. Every man who said they loved me failed me. They promised me a future with them and that we would one day have a home, children and a normal life. All of these promises never came true. They would leave me saying I will be back and they never kept their word. I could not trust what a man said. This type of love they gave me was without hope. All it gave me was a life of destruction. I thought I could not do without a love relationship.

"Put to death, therefore, whatever belongs to your earthly nature: sexual immorality, impurity, lust, evil desires and greed, which is idolatry" Colossians 3:5 (NIV).

Christians should date before marriage to become more acquainted with each other, to learn each other's talents and to learn what they want out of life. Never should dating include sexual immorality.

Proverbs 31 Woman

"Who can find a virtuous woman? for her price is far above rubies. [30]Favour is deceitful, and beauty is vain: but a woman that feareth the LORD, she shall be praised"

Proverbs 31:10 & 30 (KJV).

"There are many ways I can be more of a Proverbs 31 Woman to my husband. God is teaching me I should trust my husband more. I will continue to be more honest to him. God has taught me that I must plan my household in different steps. I must allow God to discipline me and to teach me how to buy the proper food and clothing for my family, to allow God to teach me how to spend money, putting some away for keepsakes. God has taught me to be submissive to my husband. God has given me courage to share my thoughts with him and for me not to shut myself out from him. God has given me a desire to love him for better or worse. God has taught me to speak with wisdom and to love wisdom because wisdom will be my best friend. God has taught me to share different fruit of the Spirit with Him. I have to remember what God has taught me-the beauty inside of me counts and not the vanity of the woman. God has taught me not to idolize clothes, money, and jewelry.

The Holy Spirit will help me remember to fear the Lord, because the fear of the Lord will help me be obedient to God's laws and possessions with my husband. God has taught me to continue to be humble. God has taught me to allow myself to be more confident in the things I do. God has given me His strength to accept the things I cannot change. God has taught me to put Him first and then my husband.

I would like my husband to be able to trust me and be able to confide in me of his problems. I want to have a servant's heart to my husband and to my daughter and to be able to serve him with true love from God and to remember God's strength will help me keep my household in the proper order it should be. God has given me a desire to be a godly wife to my husband. God will allow me to use the wisdom He has given me to speak the right words of gentleness and kindness. God will allow me to be patient in every circumstance that comes my way. I'm praying to God for Him to allow me to be more kind to my husband. I've asked God to help me use the gift of wisdom He has given me. God will teach me to obey His commandments, and to be able to use the laws of God in my marriage. I need God's strength to help me to be submissive to my husband's possessions, thoughts and feelings."

The Family God Made Us To Be

"I thank God for my family. My family no longer has to wonder if I'm dead or alive. God has given me a great desire to love my mother. My mother now says she loves me. God has placed so much love in my heart that I love my family unconditionally. Today, I can say I'm able to spend time with my daughter, and God has given me a mother's heart.

My daughter is the most significant person in my life. When I was pregnant with her, I felt so good inside and very special. I was so excited when she was born. I remember her as a little doll baby. She was just adorable; her skin was the color of copper. Her eyes were blue; she was very tiny. She began moving around in a walker at the age of three months. She was always the baby I wanted. She was my love child.

When she began walking, she was a walking doll. Her eyes had such a pretty innocent look, a perfect child. As she grew older, she wanted to wear dresses and skirts; she was very dainty *little girl. My child was an out going child. She was a member of the Brownies and the Girls Scouts. Cheerleading was one of her skills along with her academics, she received As and Bs in school. She had a love for going to church and Sunday school.*

I became very protective over her as a young lady. I just didn't want to accept the fact that she was growing up. And yet, her love for me never changed! Now a mother herself, I am most proud that she can stand on her own; I don't have to worry about her for she and my grandson have God today in their lives.

Before I gave my life to Christ, I couldn't enjoy my grandson. Now when I see him, I'm able to play with him and also to share the joy and love God has given me. My mom means the world to me. God has given me patience to take time with her because of her handicap. I thank God I have a sister that I love, and we are the best of friends. God has given me a burden for my favorite aunt; I love my aunt because she has a mother's heart for me. Now I can be there for my family when they need me as long as it is in the will of God.

I love my three brothers dearly. My relationship with them is a blessing. God's love for them makes the difference in our lives. God has given me a grateful heart, and I count my blessings everyday."

Almost everyone has relatives, family of some kind. Family relationships are so important in God's eyes, all members are responsible for one another; if not, they shouldn't call themselves Christians.

If our faith in Christ is real, it will usually prove itself at home, in our relationships with those who know us best. Children and parents have a responsibility to each other. Children should honor their parents even if the parents are demanding and unfair. Parents should care gently for their children, even if the children are disobedient and unpleasant. Ideally, of course, Christian parents and Christian children will relate to each other with thoughtfulness and love. This will happen if both parents and children put the others' interests above their own-that is, if they submit to one another.

Christian Stewardship

"The testing of my faith will strengthen me to endure trials and tribulations of many kinds. If I do not wait on God, I can get into trouble. God wants me to walk blamelessly and I must never become impatient. God has taught me I can never rush the manifestation of the Holy Spirit. I have learned I must continue to discipline myself in reading the Word, having a prayer life, and a personal devotion, which will give me a godly balance of time. Jesus took time off to relax, and I have learned it is all right to take time out for relaxation. God has sunsets and parks to let me sit and enjoy His creation. God has taught me the only way I can continue to understand time, is for me to continue to exercise the gift of faith. I must strive harder and press toward the mark."

The proper use of time has a lot to do with the shaping of each Christian. There is no short way of living a holy life; one must do well with God in order to serve Him. God gives all His people hardships, long suffering, testing, trials and tribulations, which are necessary, so they can develop a strong character of faith, a servant's heart.

Pursuit To Holiness

"I have learned, I can walk in obedience to God's Word and live a life of holiness. Obedience is orientated toward God and victory is orientated toward self. I have learned God will not accept

excuses or even a deviation from His perfect will. God's grace will strengthen me in my weakness. God continues to show me I can do all things through Him who gives me strength. I know today I must work out my salvation with fear and trembling. I have learned the more I read the Word of God, the more His Word becomes hidden in my heart, so I may not sin against Him. It is through the application of a scripture to a specific life situation that I will develop a kind of conviction to see me through temptations. Faith will enable me to claim the promise of God; it also will help me to obey the commandments of God."

"Tell the Israelites, "Above all, keep my Sabbaths, the sign between me and you, generation after generation, to keep the knowledge alive that I am the GOD who makes you holy" Exodus 31:13 (The Message).

Professing Christians must be brought to realize that the surpassing desire and demand of God for them is that of the continual pursuit and reflection of holiness. Holiness is not only expected, it is the promise birthright of every Christian. Every Christian should live a life of holiness.

CONCLUSION

1. What on earth, am I here for?

"Before I formed thee in the belly I knew thee: and before thou camest forth out of the womb I sanctified thee, and I ordained thee a prophet unto the nations" Jeremiah 1:5 (KJV). *Before my parents conceived me, God had divine knowledge concerning me because He is omniscient.* "For there is not a word in my tongue but, lo, O LORD: thou knowest it all together" Psalm 139:4 (KJV). *He tailored and designed me as one of His original masterpieces. God has put me together in a way that can't and should not be replicated. He chose every aspect of my personality, crafted every gift and talent He bestowed on me and gave special thoughts to each one of my features and traits. I was hand made by Him in my mother's womb. He custom designed me to fit a specific role in His sovereign plan.*

Through the Lord Jesus Christ I have been brought with a price. "Do you not know that your temple of the Holy Spirit, who is in you, whom you have received from? You are your not own; you were bought at a price. Therefore honor God with your body" 1 Corinthians 6:19-20 (NIV).

The Word of God also states in 1 Peter 1:2 (NIV), "Who have been chosen according to the foreknowledge of God the Father, through the sanctifying work of the Spirit, for obedience to Jesus Christ and sprinkling by his blood: Grace and peace be yours in abundance." *Even before I was born, God had sanctified (set me apart) for His glory. Through the Lord as a believer, I must maintain intimate communion with Christ* (John 15:4 (TLB).

Through the Lord, I must continue to engage in fellowship with believers (Ephesians 4:15-16 (KJV). *Through the Lord, I must continue to devote myself in prayer* (Colossians 4:2 (NIV). *I must continue to obey God's Word* (John 17:17 (NIV). *Through the Holy Spirit, I must remain sensitive to God's presence and care* (Mathew 6:25-34 (NIV).

Through Christ, my old self has been crucified (sin put to death) with Christ on the cross in order that I might believe and receive a new life in Christ (Romans 6:6 (NIV). According to Romans 6:7 &11 (NIV), *anyone who has died has been freed from sin and counted dead to sin but alive to God in Christ Jesus. Through Christ, He has given me the divine power of Him to resist sin. So, now I can live a new life in obedience to God. Through Him I can continue to obey and be filled with the Holy Spirit.* "Those who are led by the Spirit of God are sons of God" Romans 8:14 (NIV). "Do not get drunk with wine, which leads to debauchery. Instead be filled with the Spirit" Ephesians 5:18 (NIV).

Even before I was born God ordained me, He had appointed me, and He called me to the Great Commission. "Jesus came to them and said, "All authority in heaven and earth has been given to me, *Phyllis E. Jones,* "go and make disciples of all nations, baptizing them in the name of the Father and of the Son and of the Holy Spirit, teaching them to obey everything I have commanded you. And surely I am with you always, to the age" Mathew 28:18-20 (NIV). *God has given me divine authority to set the captives free.* "The Spirit of the Sovereign Lord is on me because the Lord has anointed me to preach good news to the poor. He has sent me to bind up the brokenhearted, to proclaim freedom for captives and release from darkness for the prisoners, to proclaim the year of the Lord's favor and the vengeance of our God, to comfort all who mourn, and provide for those who grieve in Zion—to bestow on them a crown of beauty instead of ashes, the oil of gladness instead of mourning, and a garment of praise instead of a spirit of despair. They will be called oaks of righteousness, a planting of the Lord for the display of his splendor" (Isaiah 61:1-3 (NIV).

So in conclusion of this question what on earth am I here for? God knew (approved) me and sanctified me (set me apart), and ordained (commissioned) me before I was even born. From the heart of Smith Wigglesworth, "God has a plan beyond anything that we have ever known. He has a plan for every individual life, and if we have any other plan in view, we miss the grandest plan of all. Nothing in the past is equal to the present, and nothing in the present can equal the things of tomorrow. Tomorrow should be filled with holy expectations that we will be living flames for Him. God never intended His people to be ordinary or commonplace. His intentions were that they should be on fire for Him, conscious of His divine power, realizing the glory of the Cross that foreshadows the crown." This is the desire God has given me."

What was your divine purpose at birth?

"For he chose us in him before the creation of the world to be holy and blameless in his sight. In love he predestined us to be adopted as his sons through Jesus Christ, in accordance with his pleasure and will" Ephesians 1:4-5 (NIV). *God's divine purpose for my life even before I was born-He foreknew from eternity was to love and redeem me through Christ. As a believer, I must maintain my faith in Christ so that I will not fall short of His glory. The election to salvation and holiness of the body of Christ is always certain. Christ, as the elect, is the foundation of my election. It is only in union with Christ that I became a member of the elect.*

"Here is my servant, whom I uphold, my chosen one in whom I delight, I will put my Spirit on him and he will bring justice to the nations" Isaiah 42:1 (NIV). *Through the power of the Holy Spirit, Jesus was raised from the grave and thereby vindicated as the true Messiah and the Son of God. Just as Jesus depended on the Holy Spirit for his resurrection, I as a believer must continue to depend on the Holy Spirit for spiritual life now and bodily resurrection in the future. It is only through the anointing of the Holy Spirit I can minister with the necessary wisdom, revelation and power.*

"But now listen, O Jacob, my servant, Israel, whom I have chosen. This is what the Lord says—he who made you, who formed you in the womb, and who will help you" Isaiah 44:1-2 (NIV). *God chose me even before I was born be to a servant of the Most High God. Lucifer knew God marked me, so he tried everything in his power to destroy me and to kill me. I thank God each day because what Lucifer tried for evil, being a chosen vessel, God had a divine purpose for my life. He brought me up from the grave; He spared me from going down into the pit. He has turned my weeping into rejoicing. He has turned my wailing into dancing. He removed my sackcloth and He has clothed me with His joy that my heart may sing to Him and not be silent. I will thank the Lord for the rest of my life. God has taught me that I was born to glorify Him. Christ will present me "holy and blameless in sight" only if I continue in faith. I thank God; He has predestined me as one of His elect to be:*

"And those he predestined, he also called, those he called, he also justified, those he also justified, he also glorified" Romans 8:30 (NIV). "For those God foreknew he also predestined to be conformed to the likeness of his Son, that he might be the firstborn among many brothers" Romans 8:29 (NIV).

"For he chose, Phyllis E. Jones, in him before the creation of the world to be holy and blameless in his sight to be adopted as his daughter through Jesus Christ in accordance with his good pleasure and will to the praise of his glorious grace which he has given, Phyllis E. Jones, in the One he loves" Ephesians 1:4-6 (NIV).

I thank God, He has redeemed me through His blood. As recorded in Ephesians 1:7 (NIV), "in him I have redemption through his blood, the forgiveness of sin, in accordance with the riches of God's grace." *I am God's workmanship created in Christ Jesus to do good works which God prepared in advance for me to do* Ephesians 2:10 (NIV).

In the words of Donald C. Stamp, "Concerning election and predestination, we might use the analogy of a great ship on its way to heaven. The ship (church) is chosen by God to be his very own vessel. Christ is the Captain and Pilot of this ship. All who desire to be a part of this elect ship and its Captain can do so through a living faith in Christ, by which they come on board the ship. As long as they are on the ship, in company with the ship's Captain, they are among the elect. If they choose to abandon the ship and Captain, they cease to be part of the elect. Election is always only in union with the Captain and his ship. Predestination tell us about the ship's destination and what God has prepared for those remaining on it. God invites everyone to come aboard the elect ship through faith in Jesus Christ.

I'VE BEEN REDEEMED

"Praise The Lord,

First of all, I give God All Of The Honor and all the praise because He is worthy to be praised.

Hi! My name is Phyllis and I am a Child of the Most High. I have a daughter and a grandson. God has set me free from a twenty-three year drug addiction of heroine, methadone and cocaine. I was bound in all types of sin, but today I can say I have been washed by the Blood of the Lamb! "Whom the Son has set free, is free indeed!"

Rejection played a very important part all of my life. My family gave me material things, but all I wanted was love. At the age of thirteen, I began to smoke cigarettes, drink beer, and smoke marijuana even though I was raised in the church from the age of five to the age of nineteen. Rebellion caused me to hang with the older crowd and men for love and acceptance. At the age of sixteen, I began to use heroine and cocaine, living a fast life. At age nineteen, I began to mainline drugs and drink methadone. Shooting galleries, bars, and crack houses became a part of my world. I was unable to hold on to the good jobs I had or to utilize the education and courses I had taken. It seemed as though I lacked the desire to pursue my career. There was a deep void in my life.

Three years ago I became very ill and Satan was telling me there was no hope. I became homeless, sleeping in cars, hanging out waiting for the cop man to wake me up. I was a walking zombie. Having no love for myself I was unable to love anyone. My heart was hardened. On many occasions I felt myself beginning to overdose and I would call on the Lord, singing the song "Precious Lord."

I thank God He stepped in my life and intervened. Through the power of the Holy Spirit and intercessory prayers of my family, I came to Teen Challenge. That is where I met my Lord and Savior Jesus Christ. I would like to give special thanks to Moms and I thank God she never gave up on me. I love you. A special thanks to my sister, who gave me support and love. I love you. To my aunt and my brother and his family, I thank you for your support and I love you. To (my counselor), God has placed a special love in my heart for you. To all the Saints of Teen Challenge, thank you for helping me mature in different areas of my life. I love you with the love of the Lord.

I thank God I am a new creation in Christ. Today I can walk with my head up high and not be ashamed of my old life. I have a Father that loves me. Luke 1:37, "For there is nothing impossible with God." God has filled the void in my life. He has given me the peace that surpasses all understanding, His love that will never fail, and the joy of the Lord is my strength. God has given me a grateful heart. I thank God for His mercy and His grace. God's grace is sufficient in my life. Today, I have a hope and a future. Jeremiah 29:11, "For I know the plans I have for you, declares the Lord, plans to prosper you and not to harm you plans to give you a hope and a future." God has opened doors for me with employment and the Re-entry Program here at Teen Challenge. Soon I will be finishing my education and attending Bible School. The biggest goal in my life, if it is the will of the Lord, is to start an HIV Ministry. I will always apply these two scriptures to my life; 1 John 4:4 "You, dear children, are from God and have overcome them, because the one who is in you is greater than the one who is in the world" and Philippians 4:13, "I can do everything through Him who gives me strength."

Christ has redeemed us from the curse of the law! "Christ hath redeemed us from the curse of the law, being made a curse for us: for it is written, Cursed is every one that hangeth on a tree: That the blessing of Abraham might come on the Gentiles through Jesus Christ; that we might receive the promise of the Spirit through faith. And if ye be Christ's, then are ye Abraham's seed, and heirs according to the promise" (Galatians 3:13-14 & 29).

Some people would have us believe that we don't have any promise in this life of any blessing material or otherwise. Almost every time you get something good from the Word of God, or the promise of something good and a Scripture to stand on, someone pops up and says, that's just for the Jews. Abraham's blessing belongs to us (Galatians 3:14, 29). It doesn't belong only to the physical descendents of Abraham; it belongs to us! Abraham's blessing is ours! They can't take it away from us anymore. Those doubters, unbelievers, joy killers, and doubt peddlers will not be able to take it away from us.

Redemption begins in a true deliverance from a vain manner of life, from a life of sin. The word itself includes everything God does for a sinner from the pardon of sin, in which it begins (Ephesians 1:14; 4:30) to the full deliverance of the body by resurrection "For all have sinned, and come short of the glory of God; being justified freely by his grace through the redemption that is in Christ Jesus" (Romans 3:23-24).

Bibliography

Augsburger, David *Caring Enough To Confront*

Backus, William & Candace *Untwisting Twisted Relationships*

Guyon, Madame *Experiencing God Through Prayer*

Mc Clung, Jr., Floyd *The Father Heart of God*

Mc Dowell, Josh *Find The Treasure In You*

Meyer, F. B. *Changed By The Master's Touch*

Murray, Andrew *Waiting On God*

Philips, Bob *Developing Christian Character*

Torres, Ben *Preparing for A Spiritual Change*

Torres, Ben *The Process Of Bearing Fruit*

Torres, Ben *The Renewing Of The Mind*

Torres, Ben *How God Uses Circumstances*

Torres, Ben *God's Pressure Cooker*

Torres, Ben *Reigning With Christ*

Torres, Ben *Deliverance From The Self-Life*

Torres, Ben *Deliverance From The Work Of The Devil*

Torres, Ben *Deliverance From The Power Of Sin*

Torres, Ben *Deliverance From The Old Creation*

Torres, Ben *The Scripture & The Addict*

Van-Stone, Dori *The Girl Nobody Loved*

Van-Stone, Dori *No Place To Cry*

Wilkerson, David *Have You Given Up Lately*

BIBLE CITATIONS

ABOUT THE AUTHOR

Prophetess Dr. Phyllis Elizabeth Jones-Coleman, a native of NJ, is a God-fearing woman. She is a mother, grandmother and wife, married to Deacon Leon Coleman Sr. residing in Brooklyn, NY.

Her strength and dignity does not come from her amazing achievements, however; they are a result of her reverence for God the Father and a intimate and personal relationship with Jesus Christ our Savior. She is a soilder in the Army Of the Lord, who is sold out to the Lord.

Prophetess Dr. Coleman is a graduate of Teen Challenge Disiciple Ministry Brooklyn, NY. Employment with the Bedford Stuyvesant Mental Health Department with Favor of God resting on her life, launched her career in the The Research Foundation \The State University of New York. As a counselor\teacher at Teen Challenge since January 1995.

She continued her education at the Open Faith Bilbe College and Seminary of NY and the International Seminary and Bible College of California, receiving a Bachelor of Theology, major in ChristianCounseling\ Psychology in 1999, that year she was license as a minister.. Under the same toolage of Dr. Terrance Parris she received a Master of Theology, majoring in Christian Counseling/ Psychology in 2001 which God allowed her to become a ordain minister in 2005. Dr Phyllis Coleman received a Doctorate Degree of Divinity in June 2005. The Holy Spirit gave her the desire to study and know the mystery of Christ, so Dr. Phyllis Coleman in June 7, 2008 received her PHD Degree of Philosophy in Pastoral Psychology from the Open Bilbe College and Seminary of NY and American International University. Because God continue to move by His Spirit and her love, obedience and to the Father, the Spirit the of the Lord has taken her to a new level as a prophetess of God, she was ordained June 7, 2008. The International Board of Christian Counselors on Feb. 2, 2009 has embraced Dr. Phyllis Coleman with her credentials as a Board Certified Pastoral Counselor.

Dr. Phyllis Coleman is the Executive Director and Founder of the Woman at the Well World wide Inc. Currently, she is under the office of a prophet at Greater Level Hill Baptist Church in the city of Newark, NJ Pastor Silas Dunell. This power-packed Prophet of God preaches\teaches the uncompromised end time Word of God in power and demonstration.